Fodor's

brussels

Excerpted from *Fodor's Belgium and Luxembourg*

fodor's travel publications
new york • toronto • london • sydney • auckland
www.fodors.com

contents

maps

ON THE ROAD WITH FODOR'S

EVERY TRIP IS A SIGNIFICANT TRIP. Acutely aware of that fact, we've pulled out all stops in preparing Fodor's Pocket Brussels 1st Edition. To guide you in putting together your Brussels experience, we've created multiday itineraries and regional tours. And to direct you to the places that are truly worth your time and money, we've rallied the team of endearingly picky know-it-alls we're pleased to call our writers. Having seen all corners of Brussels, they're real experts. If you knew them, you'd poll them for tips yourself.

Leslie Adler is a Brussels-based journalist with an international news organization. After living on both the East and West coasts and the Midwest of America, she moved to London in 1995, and to Brussels in 1998. She's written extensively about Belgium and the long-standing divide between the Dutch-speaking Flemish and French-speaking Walloons. "I love traveling and exploring new places, and living in Europe has allowed me to indulge that passion. As a journalist in Brussels, I continually find new challenges in trying to understand the Belgian mentality." For this book she contributed to the Here and There, Shopping, and Outdoor Activities and Sports chapters.

Brussels native **Eric R. Drosin** has traveled throughout Europe, the United States, and Africa, but Belgium's appeal has never flagged. He worked as a copy editor at The Wall Street Journal Europe for five years before joining the Dow Jones Newswires Brussels bureau as a journalist covering E.U. agriculture, environment, and health and consumer safety issues. He lent his expertise to the Side Trips chapter here.

Barbara Jacobs, a Philadelphia native, first visited Belgium—her first taste of continental Europe—as a girl in 1967. She vowed to return, and 10 years later accepted a two-year assignment as a translator at the U.S. Embassy in Brussels. Before the two years had ended, Belgium had become her home, and she has lived there ever since. Through her Belgian husband, she has gained insight to the understated richness of the region's culture and humor. She shares her knowledge and appreciation of the heart of Europe in Practical Information.

London-born **Katharine Mill** moved to Belgium in 1998, having previously taught English at Bordeaux University, France, and completed her studies at Bristol University, England. A keen cyclist (and former coeditor of the official guide to the Tour de France), she was drawn by the country's reputation in the two-wheeled world. Now deputy editor of Brussels's English-language weekly magazine, The Bulletin, she thinks the capital of Europe has everything a city needs—yet remarkably few of the drawbacks. For this book she reviews the high points of its dining, lodging, and nightlife.

Don't Forget to Write

Keeping a travel guide fresh and up-to-date is a big job. So we love your feedback—positive and negative—and follow up on all suggestions. Contact the Brussels editor at editors@fodors.com or c/o Fodor's, 280 Park Avenue, New York, NY 10017. And have a wonderful trip!

Karen Cure

Editorial Director

North Sea

Westerschelde

Kal...

Knokke-Heist

Zeebrugge

Blankenberge

Oostende

Beveren

Nieuwpoort

E40

N9

Brugge (Bruges)

Maldegem

N49

Sint-Niklaas

De Panne

EAST FLANDERS

N70

Veurne

Diksmuide

E40

A17

N35

Deinze

Gent (Ghent)

E17

Dendermo...

Roeselare

Aalst

WEST FLANDERS

Ieper

A19

A47/A14

Kortrijk

Oudenaarde

BRUS...

N42

Geraards-bergen

Gaasbeek

N8

Bee...

Ronse

Halle

Schelde

A8

N7

Ath

Enghien

Soignies

A8

Ror...

N6

E19

Tournai

HAINAULT

N56

Beloeil

la Louvière

Mons

Binc...

E19

Sambre

C...

FRANCE

N

0   20 miles

0   30 km

Essen

mthout

NETHERLANDS

ANTWERP (PROVINCE)

Antwerpen (Antwerp)

Beerse

Turnhout

Arendonk

Lommel

Herentals

Geel

Olen

Lier

Westerlo

Mechelen

Keerbergen

Diest

Aarschot

onde

Leuven

Zoutleeuw

BRABANT

Bruxelles (Brussels)

rsel

Jodoigne

Tienen

Sint Truiden

Waterloo

KEMPEN

LIMBURG

Bree

Genk

Hasselt

Tongeren

Liège

GERMANY

quières

Nivelles

Huy

Meuse

Ourthe

LIEGE (PROVINCE)

Spa

Malmedy

Gosselies

Namur

Charleroi

Yvoir

Dinant

Anhée

NAMUR (PROVINCE)

Durbuy

ARDENNES

La Roche-en-Ardenne

Thuin

eaumon

Philippeville

Rochefort

Han-sur-Lesse

LUXEMBOURG (PROVINCE)

Bastogne

Chimay

Meuse

Bouillon

Neufchâteau

Arlon

LUXEMBOURG

brussels

In This Chapter

introducing brussels

BRUSSELS (BRUXELLES IN FRENCH, BRUSSEL IN FLEMISH) is a provincial city at heart, even after it assumed a new identity as capital of the European Union (EU) in 1958. Within Belgium, Brussels has equal status with Flanders and Wallonia as an autonomous region. It's a bilingual enclave just north of the language border that divides the country into Flemish- and French-speaking parts. Historically, it's also the capital of Flanders.

At the end of the 19th century, Brussels was one of Europe's liveliest cities, known for its splendid cafés and graceful art nouveau architecture. That gaiety, however, was stamped out by German occupation during the First and Second World Wars. Still, the city made a comeback little more than a decade later, its reemergence on the international scene heralded by the World's Fair and the Universal Exposition of 1958.

As a by-product of Europe's increasing integration, international business has invaded the city since the 1960s. The result: blocks of steel-and-glass office buildings set just steps from cobbled-street neighborhoods. Over the centuries, Brussels has been shaped by the different cultures of the foreign powers that have ruled it. It has learned the art of accommodating them and, in the process, prepared itself for its role as the political capital of Europe.

PORTRAITS

LES MOULES SONT ARRIVÉES!

Damp and cold mist the leaded-glass windows, but inside the café glows a scene worthy of a Flemish Master. The burnished wooden banquettes are Rembrandt's; the lace curtain, Vermeer's. Hals would have painted the diner, a lone bearded man in rumpled black leather and heavy, worn wool, his thick fingers clasping a broad-stemmed bowl of mahogany-brown beer. Before him lies a spread of crockery and mollusks, a still-life in themselves: The two-quart pot is heaped high with blue-black mussels, their shells flecked with bits of onion and celery, the broth beneath them steaming; beside them a bowl piled high with yellow *frites* (french fries), crisp and glistening; in the corner, a saucer of slabs of floury-gold cracked-wheat bread. The man works studiously, absorbed in a timeless ritual: Fish out the shell from the broth with fingers inured to the heat by years of practice. Pluck out the plump flesh with a fork and, while chewing the morsel, chuck the shell aside on a crockery plate. Sometimes he sets down the fork and uses the empty shell as pincers to draw out the meat of the next shell. As the meal progresses, the pile in the pot shrinks and the heap of empty shells grows. As the beer follows the mussels, its strong tonic paints the man's cheeks until two ruby patches radiate above his beard. The painting's caption: "Man eating moules."

It is the central image of the Flemish lowlands—the Netherlands, Flanders, even leaking into landlocked Wallonie and Luxembourg.

But this warmly lit interior scene wouldn't be as striking without its harsh exterior foil: Mussels, like the Dutch and the Flemish, are creatures of the sea; they flourish in cold, inky waters along rock-crusted shores, clustered and stacked like blue-black crystals in muddy tidal pools. They're a product of caustic sea winds and briny, chilly damp, and their bite tastes like salt air itself.

Most of the mussels consumed in the Benelux region come from the North Sea, above all in the Waddenzee, off the northern coast of the Netherlands. Captured by the billions in great nets along the bottom of specially protected, fenced-off nursery beds, they are sorted by weight and auctioned to wholesalers in Zeeland, who return them to shallow tidal waters to recover from the trip, to mature, and to purge themselves of sandy mud. From there, they are harvested en masse and shipped live across Europe.

The cultivation of mussels dates from Roman times, though legend credits an Irish shipwreck victim who settled in La Rochelle, on the west coast of France; he is said to have noticed great colonies of the mollusks clinging to posts he planted to hold fishing nets. By placing posts closer together and arranging branches between them, he was able to create an ideal breeding ground and, in essence, mass-produce the delicacy. (The French, predictably enough, prefer their own, smaller mussels from the coasts of Brittany and Normandy, insisting that North Sea mussels are fleshy, dull, and vulgarly oversized.)

Scrubbed with stiff brushes under running water, soaked with salt to draw out the sand, and often fed flour to plump and purge them, mussels are served throughout the region in dozens of ways. The building block for French or Walloon recipes: simmering them à la marinière, in a savory stock of white wine, shallots, parsley, and butter. It's difficult to improve on this classic method, which brings out the best in mussels' musky sea essence—but chefs have been trying for centuries. Another common version is à la crème, the marinière stock thickened with flour-based white sauce and a generous portion of heavy cream. Flemish mussels, on the other hand, are nearly always served in a simple, savory vegetable stock, with bits of celery, leek, and onions creeping into the shells. The Dutch have been known to pickle them, or even to fry them in batter. Those who don't want to get their fingers messy may order their mussels *meunière*, removed from the shells in the kitchen and baked in a pool of garlicky butter. Regardless of the preparation, the Belgians and the Dutch wash their mussels down with beer, the Luxembourgers with an icy bottle of one of the coarser Moselle wines—an Elbling or a Rivaner.

Mussels rations are anything but stingy here, and on your first venture you may be appalled by the size of the lidded pot put before you. It's the shells that create the volume, and once you've plucked out the tender flesh, thrown away the shells, and sipped the broth and succulent strays from a colossal soup spoon, you'll soon find yourself at the bottom of the pot. Don't worry: Many restaurants will whisk it away and come back with Round Two— another mountain of the steamy blue creatures, another pool of savory broth. It's called *moules à volonté* (all you can eat), so gird yourself for a feast: The locals have been doing it for 2,000 years.

— Nancy Coons

FROM PILSNER TO PEACHES

Although Belgium's microbrewing industry is declining as the giant Interbrew firm flexes its muscles, beer is still the national beverage. The traditional Belgian sits at a café table and sips a beer that was chosen thoughtfully from a lengthy list and poured with considerable care into the appropriate type of glass.

If you want an ordinary glass of beer, ask for *un export*, or pilsner *un pils*, a light, palatable brew. Lambic ales, made with part wheat and part barley, include the syrup-sweetened, fruity Kriek; the raspberry flavored pink Framboise; the peach flavored Peche; the Casis, which is made with black currants; and the Muscat, made with grapes. Faro and Gueuze are also Lambic ales without the fruity edge. Witbier is a white, frothy beer made only from wheat.

Many Belgian monasteries brew beers, and those that follow a regulated process are know as Trappist. Orval, Chimay,

Westmalle, Westvleteren, and Rochefort are all official Trappist breweries. Their beers tend to be stronger than Lambic brews or Witbier—some have 11.5% alcohol. Westmalle coined the "triple," a decidedly strong beer.

In the bars and cafés of Brussels, you'll also find many brands from Great Britian, Germany, France, Denmark, and the Netherlands. Rest assured that the Belgian beer conaissance extends even to imports: here they insist that their Guinness come from Dublin rather than the United Kingdom.

PLEASURES AND PASTIMES

ARCHITECTURE
The flowing lines, stained-glass windows, and lavish mosaics of the city's art nouveau buildings make many streets living museums. The architectural works of the great Victor Horta grace many quarters, as do buildings by his disciples. The art deco style adopted by Horta later in his career is also in evidence.

ART
The city's art museums embrace a diversity of styles and celebrate Belgium's native artists. Traditional Flemish artists, including Pieter Bruegel the Elder, are well represented, as are the works of the surrealist René Magritte and other 20th-century artists, such as Paul Delvaux.

BÉGUINAGES
Cathedrals and béguinages highlight the city's religious history and architectural innovations. Beautiful stained-glass windows and gleaming white towers are the hallmarks of the renovated, 13th-century Cathédrale St-Michel et Ste-Gudule in the heart of town. In the same neighborhood, the Flemish Baroque Eglise St-Jean-du-Béguinage and the 1,000-year-old Eglise St-Nicolas give you a glimpse into lives of the Beguines.

DINING

Your dining experience may take place inside a grand town house with baroque glam or a former factory that's the epitome of minimalist chic. Regardless of the setting, decor, or cuisine, the quality of food is consistently high.

LODGING

Although family-run hostelries and designer-label lodgings are almost nonexistent, there are a variety of quirky, old-world places. Consider a stay in one of the many Belle Epoque hostels, which were occupied during the war, abandoned mid-century, and then brought back to center stage. Such hotels offer the charms of a bygone era alongside information-age amenities.

MARKETS

What's for sale? Just about everything. In addition to several produce markets, you'll find a market devoted to flowers, another to birds, and still another to antiques and books. For more eclectic offerings, try the Vieux Marché flea market and the Marché du Midi bazaar.

MUSEUMS

The city's museums help to tell its many and varied tales. There are institutions devoted to military history, art deco and art nouveau, beer brewing, musical instruments, vintage cars, fine and modern art, central African culture, and Belgian folklore.

SQUARES

You can wander through plaza after plaza on a tour of the popular attractions. These busy squares are landmarks, rest stops, and as shopping hubs. Some have bustling markets; others feature historic structures. The most famous is the Place du Grand Sablon, an elegant, shop- and café-surrounded hill.

NEW AND NOTEWORTHY

Brussels gleams anew in 2001, benefiting from major face-lifts to public parks and buildings. A thorough renovation of the Parc de Bruxelles overlooking the Palais du Roi has restored it to grace. Nearby, the Eglise Notre-Dame du Sablon at the eastern end of the elegant Place du Grand Sablon is luminously white. In addition to preserving its heritage, Brussels continues to add to its skyline. The European Commission's Berlaymont building is taking shape as a shining new skyscraper after years under wraps due to asbestos contamination. And Brussels's recently opened Musée des Instruments de Musique (Museum of Musical Instruments) has a world-class collection of instruments that span both the centuries and the globe.

In This Chapter

Updated by Leslie Adler

here and there

AROUND THE 1,000-YEAR-OLD historic center of Brussels, a group of ring roads form concentric circles. Crossing them is like traveling back and forth across the centuries. Brussels once had a river, the Senne, but it was buried in the 19th century after becoming clogged with sewage; the absence of left and right river banks can make orientation in the city a bit difficult.

The center, sitting in a bowl, is sometimes known as the Pentagon, from the shape of the oldest ring road, which roughly follows the ancient ramparts. The remains of the ruins include one of the gates, the Porte de Hal, the Tour Noire (Black Tower) on Place Ste-Catherine, and a small patch of wall next to a bowling alley near Place de la Chapelle. On either side of the 19th-century ring road you can see the cupolas of the Palais de Justice and the Basilique. In the center, the slender belfry of the Hôtel de Ville rises like a beacon.

Brussels is small enough that you can get a superficial impression of it from a car window in a single day. For a more substantial appreciation, however, you need one day for the historic city heart, another for the uptown squares and museums, and additional days for museums outside the center and excursions to the periphery. There are many attractive nooks and crannies to explore.

LOWER TOWN: THE HEART OF BRUSSELS

During the latter half of the 10th century, a village began to emerge on the site of present-day Brussels. A population of craftspeople and traders settled gradually around the castle of the counts of Leuven, who were later succeeded by the dukes of Brabant.

In 1430 Philip the Good, Duke of Burgundy, took possession of Brussels, then known as Brabant. During this era, Brussels became a center for the production of tapestry, lace, and other luxury goods. By 1555, when Charles V abdicated in favor of his son, Philip II of Spain, the Protestant Reformation was spreading through the Low Countries. Philip, a devout Catholic, dealt ruthlessly with advocates of the Reformation. His governor, the Duke of Alva, had the leaders of the revolt, the Counts of Egmont and Hoorn, executed on the Grand'Place. A monument to them stands in the square of the Petit Sablon.

In 1695, on the orders of French King Louis XIV, Marshal Villeroy bombarded the city with red-hot cannonballs. The ensuing fires destroyed 4,000 houses, 16 churches, and all of the Grand'Place, with the exception of the Town Hall. The buildings around the square were immediately rebuilt, in the splendor that we see today.

In 1713 the Spanish Netherlands came under the rule of the Austrian Habsburgs. Despite the influence of Enlightenment theories on the province's governors, nationalist feeling had set in among large sections of the populace. These sentiments were quashed by neither the repressive armies of Napoléon nor the post-Waterloo incorporation of Belgium into a new Kingdom of the Netherlands. On August 25, 1830, a rousing duet from an Auber opera being performed at La Monnaie inflamed patriots in the audience, who burst onto the streets and raised the flag of Brabant. With support from Britain and France, independence came swiftly.

Since then, Brussels has undergone image upheavals almost as significant as the impact of this century's two world wars. At the turn of the 20th century, the wide boulevards and sumptuous art nouveau buildings symbolized a city as bustling and metropolitan as Paris. However, from the 1950s onward, Brussels became a byword for boring: a gray, faceless city of bureaucrats where cavalier neglect of urban planning created a new word—bruxellization—for the destruction of architectural heritage. Now the pace of European integration (and the wonders of the city's food and drink) has helped to restore the city's international reputation—but internal tensions between Flemings and French-speakers still threaten to tear it apart.

Numbers in the text correspond to numbers in the margin and on the Central Brussels map.

A Good Walk

Start at Rues de l'Etuve and du Chêne at **Manneken Pis** ①, a bronze statue of a small boy urinating that symbolizes the insouciant spirit of the Bruxellois. Thousands of copies are on sale in the souvenir shops along the three blocks of Rue de l'Etuve leading to the **Grand'Place** ②, the magnificent square surrounded by the Hôtel de Ville (Town Hall) and ornate guild houses. The alley next to the Maison du Roi (opposite the Town Hall) leads into the restaurant-lined Petite Rue des Bouchers with the highly original puppet theater, **Théâtre Toone** ③, in the **Quartier de l'Ilôt Sacré** ④. Turn right at the top of the street to reach the **Galeries St-Hubert** ⑤, an impressively engineered and decorated shopping gallery from 1847.

At the exit from the gallery, turn right on Rue d'Arenberg and cross the uninspiring Boulevard de Berlaymont, heading for the twin Gothic towers of the **Cathédrale St-Michel et Ste-Gudule** ⑥, a 13th-century edifice with outstanding stained-glass windows. Walk back down the hill and turn right on Boulevard de Berlaymont. Take the second flight of stairs on the left, with a large statue of the cartoon character Gaston Lagaffe

central brussels

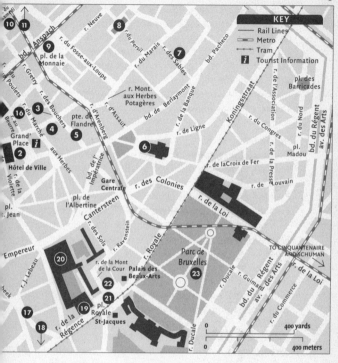

KEY

— Rail Lines
∼ Metro
∼ Tram
i Tourist Information

at the top of the stairs, down to the Rue des Sables and the
Centre Belge de la Bande Dessinée ⑦, or Belgian Comic Strip
Center, which is as engrossing to adults as it is enchanting to
kids. A left and a right take you into Rue du Persil and the **Place
des Martyrs** ⑧. Half a block away, the pedestrian shopping
street of Rue Neuve is filled with bargain-seeking shoppers in
the daytime. This street leads to the Place de la Monnaie and its
Théâtre de la Monnaie ⑨, one of Europe's leading opera
stages.

As you cross the busy Boulevard Anspach onto the Rue des
Augustins, the remnants of the **Tour Noire** ⑩ are on your left. To
the right, the short Rue des Cyprès leads to the Flemish Baroque
Eglise St-Jean-du-Béguinage ⑪. Walk down the Rue du
Peuplier and you're in the old Fish Market area—although the
canal has been replaced by ponds, and every house is now a
seafood restaurant. Turn left toward the blackened church of
Ste-Catherine and you'll find a busy market in front of it on the
Place Ste-Catherine ⑫. Take the first right, Rue de Flandre.
Halfway up the block is the gateway to the **Maison de la
Bellonne** ⑬, now a theater museum. Returning to the Place Ste-
Catherine, cross the square and take the second street on the
right. This is **Rue Antoine Dansaert** ⑭, the heart of the city's
fashionable quarter. You are now facing the grandiose stock
exchange, the **Bourse** ⑮. Next to it is Bruxella 1238, an in situ
archaeological museum, and the small **Eglise St-Nicolas** ⑯,
hemmed in by tiny houses. From where you now stand on Rue au
Beurre it's just half a block back to the Grand'Place.

TIMING

Walking the route will take you about two hours—and note that
you will need good walking shoes for the cobblestone streets.
The Grand'Place requires half an hour, more if you linger in one
of its cafés. Stops in churches and museums may add another
hour and a half. With a break for lunch, this is a comfortable,
one-day program any day of the week, especially Monday, when

museums are closed. (Most of the city's must-see museums are in the Upper Town or farther outside the center.)

Sights to See

⑮ BOURSE. At the Stock Exchange, the decorative frieze of allegorical statues in various stages of nudity—some of them by Rodin—forms a sort of idealization of the common man. Trading here, as at most European stock exchanges, is via electronic computer screens, meaning that there is no longer a trading floor. Next door lies **Bruxella 1238**, an in situ archaeological museum where you can inspect the excavation of a 13th-century church. *R. de la Bourse, tel. 02/279–4355. BF100/€2.50. Guided visits from Town Hall, Wed. 10:15, 11:15, 1:45, 2:30, 3:15.*

❻ CATHÉDRALE ST-MICHEL ET STE-GUDULE. Next to nothing is known about St. Gudule, the daughter of a 7th-century Carolingian nobleman, but this is where her relics have been preserved for the past 1,000 years. Construction of the cathedral began in 1226. Its twin Gothic towers are gleaming white again after the removal of centuries of grime. The interior was recently renovated, and the remains of an earlier, 11th-century Romanesque church that was on the site can be glimpsed through glass apertures set into the floor. Among the windows in the cathedral, designed by various artists, those by Bernard van Orley, a 16th-century court painter, are outstanding. The window of *The Last Judgment*, at the bottom of the nave, is illuminated from within in the evening. *Parvis Ste-Gudule, tel. 02/217–8345. Daily 7:30–6.*

★ ☜ ❼ CENTRE BELGE DE LA BANDE DESSINÉE. It fell to the land of Tintin, a cherished cartoon character, to create the Belgian Comic Strip Center, the world's first museum dedicated to this type of art. Despite its primary appeal to children, comic strip art has been taken seriously in Belgium for many years, and in this museum it is wedded to another strongly Belgian art form: art nouveau. The building was designed by Victor Horta in 1903 for a textile wholesaler, and the lighting and stairs, always important to

Horta, are impressive. They serve the purposes of the new owner equally well. Tintin, the creation of the late, great Hergé, became a worldwide favorite cartoon character, and his albums have sold an estimated 80 million copies. But many other artists have followed in Hergé's footsteps, some of them even more innovative. The collection includes more than 400 original plates by Hergé and his successors and 25,000 cartoon works; those not exhibited can be viewed in the archives. There's also a large comic strip shop, a library, and an attractive art nouveau brasserie. *R. des Sables 20, tel. 02/219–1980. BF250/€6.20. Tues.–Sun. 10–6.*

⑪ **EGLISE ST-JEAN-DU-BÉGUINAGE.** Originally this elegant Flemish baroque church served as the center for the *béguines* (lay sisters) who lived in houses clustered around it. The interior has preserved its Gothic elements, with soaring vaults. The surprisingly different architectural styles combine to make this one of the most attractive churches in Brussels. A number of streets converge on the small, serene, circular square, which is surrounded by buildings that help create a harmonious architectural whole. *Pl. du Béguinage. Tues.–Fri. 10–5.*

NEED A BREAK? **A la Mort Subite** (*R. Montagne-aux-Herbes-Potagères 7, tel. 02/513–1318*) is a Brussels institution named after a card game called "Sudden Death." This café, unaltered for 75 years, serves Mort Subite lambic beers on tap, in a wide range of fruit flavors.

⑯ **EGLISE ST-NICOLAS.** This small church, surrounded by tiny houses that seem to huddle under it, is almost 1,000 years old. Little remains of the original structure, but a cannonball fired by the French in 1695 is still lodged in one of the pillars. *R. au Beurre 1, tel. 02/513–8022. Weekdays 7:45–6:30, Sat. 9–6, Sun. 9–7:30; mass in English, Sun. at 10 AM.*

NEED A BREAK? **Cirio** (*R. de la Bourse 18–20, tel. 02/512–1395*) is a peaceful café with outstanding art nouveau decor that hasn't changed for generations—nor, apparently, has some of the clientele.

⑤ GALERIES ST-HUBERT. A visit to this arcade is like going shopping with your great-grandparents. There are three parts to it: *de la Reine, du Roi,* and *du Prince* (of the queen, the king, and the prince). They were built in 1847 as the world's first covered shopping galleries, thanks to new engineering techniques that allowed architects to use iron girders to design soaring constructions of glass. Neoclassical gods and heroes look down from their sculpted niches on the crowded scene below; flags of many nations billow ever so slightly; and the buskers play classical music, while diffused daylight penetrates the gallery from the glassed arches. The shops, which are generally open Monday to Saturday 10–6, are interspersed with cafés, restaurants, a theater, and a cinema. *Access from R. des Bouchers or Carrefour de l'Europe, tel. 02/512–2116.*

★ **② GRAND'PLACE.** This jewel box of a square is arguably Europe's most ornate and most theatrical. It is close to the hearts of all the people of the city, and all ages come here from time to time. At night the burnished facades of the guild houses and their gilded statuary look especially dramatic: from April to September, the square is floodlit after sundown with waves of changing colors, accompanied by music. Try to be here for the *Ommegang*, a magnificent historical pageant re-creating Emperor Charles V's reception in the city in 1549 (the first Tuesday and Thursday in July). You'll find here a daily flower market, frequent jazz and classical concerts, and in December, under the majestic Christmas tree, a life-size crèche with sheep grazing around it. *Intersection of R. des Chapeliers, R. Buls, R. de la Tête d'Or, R. au Beurre, R. Chair et Pain, R. des Harengs, and R. de la Colline.*

GUILD HOUSES OF THE GRAND'PLACE. Built in ornate baroque style soon after the 1695 bombardment, the guild houses have a striking architectural coherence. Among the buildings on the north side of the square, No. 1–2, **Le Roy d'Espagne**, belonged to the bakers' guild. It is surmounted by a cupola on which the figure of Fame is perched. **Le Sac**, No. 4, commissioned by the guild of joiners and coopers, and No. 6, **Le**

Cornet, built for the boatmen, were both designed by Antoon Pastorana, a gifted furniture maker. **Le Renard**, No. 7, was designed for the guild of haberdashers and peddlers; a sculpture of St. Christopher, their patron, stands on top of the gable. **Le Cygne**, No. 9, was formerly a butchers' guild. Today, it is an elegant restaurant, but before that it was a popular tavern often frequented by Karl Marx. *Grand'Place.*

HÔTEL DE VILLE. The Gothic Town Hall, which dates from the early 15th century, dominates the Grand'Place. Nearly 300 years older than the guild houses, which were rebuilt after the French bombardment of 1695, it was renovated most recently in 1997. The left wing was begun in 1402 but was soon found to be too small. Charles the Bold laid the first stone for the extension in 1444, and it was completed four years later. The extension left the slender belfry off center; it has now been fully restored. The belfry is topped by a bronze statue of St. Michael crushing the devil beneath his feet. Over the gateway are statues of the prophets, female figures representing lofty virtues, and effigies of long-gone dukes and duchesses. Inside the Town Hall are a number of excellent Brussels and Mechelen tapestries, some of them in the Gothic Hall, where recitals and chamber-music concerts are frequently held. *Grand'Place, tel. 02/279–4365. BF100/€2.50. Guided tours only, Tues. and Wed.: Dutch: 1:45, French 2:30, English 3:15.*

NEED A BREAK? There are plenty of cafés to choose from on Grand'Place. On the ground floor of No. 1, the vast and popular **Le Roy d'Espagne** (tel. 02/513–0807) has an open fire and solid wooden furniture.

⓭ MAISON DE LA BELLONNE. This patrician 18th-century building was named for the Roman goddess of war, whose effigy decorates the baroque facade. It often hosts concerts and dance performances. *R. de Flandre 46, tel. 02/513–3333. Free. Tues.–Fri. 10–6.*

MAISON DE LA BRASSERIE. On the same side of the Grand'Place as the Town Hall, this was once the brewers' guild. Today it houses a modest **Brewery Museum**, appropriate enough in a country that still brews 400 different beers. *Grand'Place 10, tel. 02/ 511–4987. BF100/€2.50. Daily 10–5.*

MUSÉE DU CACAO ET DU CHOCOLAT. The Museum of Cacao and Chocolate is another modest museum giving an inside look at one of Belgium's prize products. The museum explains how the cacao beans are grown and processed and takes viewers through the entire stage of chocolate production. Visitors even get a small tasting. *Grand'Place 13, tel. 02/514–2048. BF200/€4.95. Tues.–Sat. 10–5.*

MAISON DU ROI. No ruler ever lived in this House of the King; rather, it was named for its grandeur. Today, it houses the **Musée Communal**, a Municipal Museum that has some fine tapestries, altarpieces, and paintings, notably the *Marriage Procession*, by Pieter Bruegel the Elder. On the top floor you can see the extravagant wardrobe of costumes donated to clothe the little statue of *Manneken Pis* on festive occasions. *Grand'Place, tel. 02/279–4355. BF100/€2.50 for House and Museum. Tues.–Fri. 10–5, weekends 10–1.*

❶ MANNEKEN PIS. For centuries, the small bronze statue of a chubby boy urinating into a fountain has drawn visitors from near and far. (A rarely remarked-upon fact is that he is left-handed.) The first mention of him dates from 1377. Sometimes called "Brussels's Oldest Citizen," he has also been said to symbolize what Belgians think of the authorities, especially those of occupying forces. The present version was commissioned from sculptor Jerome Duquesnoy in 1619. It is a copy; the original was seized by French soldiers in 1747. In restitution, King Louis XV of France was the first to present *Manneken Pis* with a gold-embroidered suit. The statue now has 517 other costumes for ceremonial occasions, an ever-increasing collection whose recent benefactors include John Malkovich and Dennis Hopper. Thousands of copies, in various materials and sizes, are sold as souvenirs every year. A female version, the Jeanneke Pis, can be found at the Petit Sablon. *Corner of R. de l'Etuve and R. du Chêne.*

8 PLACE DES MARTYRS. This square is dedicated to the 445 patriots who died in the brief 1830 war of independence against the Dutch. The shrine to the patriots is underneath the square. The square itself is a neoclassical architectural ensemble built in 1795 in the cool style favored by the Austrian Habsburgs. This noble square has also been a martyr to local political and real estate interests, notably squabbling between the two linguistic administrations, which has hampered much-needed renovations. *R. du Persil.*

12 PLACE STE-CATHERINE. If you find the Grand'Place overrun by tourists, come to this square, a favorite of locals. It's a working market every weekday from 7 to 5, where people come to shop for necessities and banter with fishmongers. There's a stall where you can down a few oysters, accompanied by a glass of ice-cold muscadet. In the evening the action moves to the old **Vismet** (Fish Market), which branches off from the Eglise de Ste-Catherine. All that remains of the old canal is a couple of elongated ponds, but both sides are lined with seafood restaurants, some excellent, many overpriced. In good weather, there's outdoor waterside dining. *Intersection of R. Ste-Catherine, R. du Vieux Marché aux Grains, R. de Flandre, Quai aux Briques, Quai au Bois à Bruler, Pl. du Samedi, R. Plateau, and R. Melsens.*

★ **4 QUARTIER DE L'ILÔT SACRÉ.** Pickpockets, flimflam artists, and jewelry vendors mingle with the crowds in the narrow Rue des Bouchers and even narrower Petite Rue des Bouchers. Still, except for the pickpockets, it's all good-natured fun in the liveliest area in Brussels, where restaurants and cafés stand cheek by jowl, their tables spilling out onto the sidewalks. One local street person makes a specialty of picking up a heaped plate and emptying it into his bag. The waiters laugh and bring another plate. The restaurants make strenuous efforts to pull you in with huge displays of seafood and game. The quality, alas, is a different matter.

⑭ RUE ANTOINE DANSAERT. Bordering the city center and the run-down "little Chicago" district, this is the flagship street of Brussels's fashionable quarter, which extends south to the Place St-Géry. Avant-garde boutiques sell Belgian-designed men's and women's fashions along with more familiar high-fashion names. There are also inexpensive restaurants, cozy bars and cafés, avant-garde galleries, and stylish furniture shops.

⑨ THÉÂTRE DE LA MONNAIE. It was here, during a performance of Auber's *La Muette de Portici* on August 25, 1830, that some members of the audience became so inflamed by the duet "Amour sacré de la patrie" that they stormed out and started a riot that led to independence. The pleasing hall, on the **Place de la Monnaie**, is among Europe's leading opera stages. *Between De Brouckere and Fossé aux Loups at R. Neuve and R. des Fripiers, tel. 02/ 218–1202.*

③ THÉÂTRE TOONE. An old puppet theater, now run by José Geal— a seventh-generation member of the Toone family who's thus known as Toone VII—this theater has a repertory of 33 plays, including some by Shakespeare. You won't understand a word, as performances are given in the local *vloms* dialect, but it's fun anyway. There's a puppet museum (only accessible during the shows) and a bar with great, old-fashioned ambience. *Impasse Schuddeveld, off Petite R. des Bouchers, tel. 02/511–7137 or 02/513– 7486. Performance BF400/€9.95; entrance to museum free with show. Performance most evenings at 8:30.*

⑩ TOUR NOIRE. Part of the 12th-century fortifications, the Black Tower is now regrettably being assimilated into the structure of a chain hotel. *Pl. Ste-Catherine.*

- -

OFF THE
BEATEN
PATH

CHÂTEAU ROYAL DE LAEKEN – Home to the Belgian royal family, the Royal Castle of Laeken was built in 1784 in a 160-hectare park north of central Brussels. The extensive royal greenhouses, built in 1902 and home to a lush collection of exotic plants, are open to the public for two weeks in April and May. The castle and park are only open to visitors during greenhouse tours; dates are set each year in February. Contact the Brussels Tourist Office for more information. *Av. Jules Van Praet 44, no phone.*

LA TOUR JAPONAISE – King Leopold II was so impressed by a Japanese structure constructed for the 1900 Paris Exhibition that he bought the plans for the 125-ft Japanese Tower and had a replica built on the edge of royal estate at Laeken. The wood doors and sculpted panels are the work of Japanese craftsmen, and the building houses temporary exhibits related to Japan. *Av. Jules Van Praet 44, tel. 02/268–1608. BF80/€2.00. Tues.–Sun 10–4:30 Laeken, or trams 52, 92.*

PAVILLON CHINOIS – Adjacent to the Japanese Tower, King Leopold had constructed the Chinese Pavillion, originally intended to house a deluxe restaurant. The kiosk and most exterior woodwork were made in Shanghai. The building is home to a collection of 17th- and 18th-century Chinese porcelain and furniture. *tel. 02/268–2538. BF80/€2.00; combined Tower and Pavillion tickets BF120/€2.95. Tues.–Sun. 10–4:30.*

- -

UPPER TOWN: ROYAL BRUSSELS

Uptown Brussels bears the hallmarks of two rulers, Austrian Charles of Lorraine and Leopold II, Belgium's empire builder. The 1713 Treaty of Utrecht, which distributed bits of Europe like pieces in a jigsaw puzzle at the end of one of the continent's many wars, handed the Low Countries to Austria. Fortunately for the Belgians, the man Austria sent here as governor was a tolerant visionary who oversaw the construction of a new palace, the neoclassical Place Royale, and other buildings that transformed the Upper Town.

The next large-scale rebuilding of Brussels was initiated by Leopold II, the second king of independent Belgium, in the latter part of the 19th century. Cousin of Queen Victoria and the Kaiser, he annexed the Congo for Belgium and applied some of the profits to grand urban projects. Present-day Brussels is indebted to him for its wide avenues and thoroughfares.

Numbers in the text correspond to numbers in the margin and on the Central Brussels map.

A Good Walk

Start at the **Place du Grand Sablon** ⑰, window-shopping at its overpriced antiques stores and often unadventurous galleries. Cross the Rue de la Régence into its sister square, the peaceful **Place du Petit Sablon** ⑱, whose formal garden is filled with, and surrounded by, statuary. Turn right on the Rue de la Régence to the **Musée d'Art Ancien** ⑲, which holds many Old Masters, and the spectacular **Musée d'Art Moderne** ⑳, which burrows underground for space to show its modern and contemporary art.

You're now on the gleaming white **Place Royale** ㉑, a pearl of 18th-century neoclassicism, with the Eglise de St-Jacques. Walk down the Rue de la Montagne du Cour; on the left is the elegant courtyard of the Palace of Charles de Lorraine. On the right is the new **Musée des Instruments de Musique** ㉒, housed in the art nouveau building that was originally home to the Old England department store. Continue along the Rue Ravenstein around Victor Horta's **Palais des Beaux-Arts,** the city's principal concert venue, and up the handsome steps to the formal **Parc de Bruxelles** ㉓. At its end, on the right, stands Leopold II's vast, hulking **Palais du Roi.**

Returning to Place Royale, pass through the gateway on the corner next to the church, and up the Rue de Namur to the Porte de Namur. You have now reached the city's most expensive shopping area. As you walk right on the Boulevard de Waterloo, you'll pass the same high-fashion names that you find in Paris, London, and New York. The focus of the shopping district is the **Place Louise** ㉔, with the avenue and gallery of the same name.

For a fitting finale, walk down the short Rue des Quatre Bras toward the looming, oppressive **Palais de Justice** ㉕. The balustrade facing the old town has a panoramic view of the city: from the cupola of the Koekelberg Basilica, the world's fifth-largest church, on the left to the Atomium, the replica of a vastly enlarged molecule, on the right. Walk down the steps to explore the colorful neighborhood of **Les Marolles** ㉖, where many of Brussels's immigrants have settled. Less than 1 km (½ mi) northwest along Boulevard du Midi is where the colorful **Kermesse du Midi** ㉗ carnival is held in summer.

TIMING

Walking time, without stopping, is about an hour and a half. For stops in the art museums (closed Monday) add another two to three hours, plus one hour for window shopping in the Grand Sablon and Place Louise areas.

Sights to See

㉗ **KERMESSE DU MIDI.** From mid-July until the end of August, all of Belgium's carnival barkers and showmen and their carousels, ghost trains, Ferris wheels, shooting galleries, rides, swings, and merry-go-rounds congregate along the Boulevard du Midi for this giant and hugely popular funfair. It extends for blocks and blocks. *Both sides of Bd. du Midi, from Pl. de la Constitution to Porte d'Anderlecht. Attractions separately priced.* 10 AM–midnight.

㉖ **LES MAROLLES.** If the Grand'Place stands for old money, the Marolles neighborhood stands for old—and current—poverty. Walk down the steps in front of the Palais de Justice and you have arrived. This was home to the workers who produced the luxury goods for which Brussels was famous. There may not be many left who still speak the old Brussels dialect, mixing French and Flemish with a bit of Spanish thrown in, but the area still has raffish charm, although gentrification is in progress. The Marolles has welcomed many waves of immigrants, the most recent from Spain, North Africa, and Turkey. Many come to the daily **Flea Market** at the Place du Jeu de Balle, where old clothes are sold along with every kind of bric-a-brac, plain junk, and the occasional gem. *Center: R. Haute and R. Blaes. Bordered by Bd. du Midi, Bd. de Waterloo heading southwest from Palais de Justice, and imaginary line running west from Pl. de la Chapelle to Bd. Maurice Lemonnier.*

★ ⑲ **MUSÉE D'ART ANCIEN.** In the first of the interconnected art museums, the Fine Arts Museum pays special attention to the great, so-called Flemish Primitives of the 15th century, who invented the art of painting with oil. The Spanish and the Austrians pilfered some of the finest works, but there's plenty left by the likes of Memling, Petrus Christus, and Rogier Van der Weyden. The collection of works by Pieter Bruegel the Elder is outstanding; it includes *The Fall of Icarus*, in which the figure of the mythological hero disappearing in the sea is but one detail of a scene in which people continue to go about their business. A century later Rubens, Van Dyck, and Jordaens dominated the art scene; their works are on the floor above. The 19th-century collection on the ground floor includes the melodramatic *Death of Marat* by Jacques-Louis David, who, like many other French artists and writers, spent years of exile in Belgium. *R. de la Régence 3, tel. 02/508–3211. BF150/€3.70. Tues.–Sun. 10–5.*

★ ⑳ **MUSÉE D'ART MODERNE.** Rather like New York's Guggenheim Museum in reverse, the Modern Art Museum burrows underground and circles downward eight floors. You can reach it by an underground passage from the Fine Arts Museum or you can enter it from the house on Place Royale where Alexandre Dumas (*père*) once lived and wrote. The collection is strong on Belgian and French art of the past 100 years, including Belgian artists who have acquired international prominence, such as the Expressionist James Ensor and the Surrealists Paul Delvaux and René Magritte, as well as Pierre Alechinsky and sculptor Pol Bury. Note that lunch hours at this and the Musée d'Ancien are staggered so as not to inconvenience visitors. *Pl. Royale 1, tel. 02/508–3211. BF150/€3.70. Tues.–Sun. 10–5.*

MUSÉE DE LA DYNASTIE. The Dynasty Museum traces the relatively short history of the Belgian royal family, since the country's independence from the Netherlands in 1830. *Place Palais 7, tel. 02/511–5578. Free. Tues.–Sun. 10–6.*

㉒ MUSÉE DES INSTRUMENTS DE MUSIQUE. The first-rate Museum of Musical Instruments opened in 1999, bringing together under one roof a collection of more than 7,000 international musical instruments from the past five centuries. The site combines the former Old England department store, designed by architect Paul Saintenoy in 1899 and one of the city's most beautiful art nouveau buildings, and the adjoining neoclassical Barré-Guimard building from 1913. A third building in the adjoining Rue Villa Hermosa houses the instrument reserve. The four-story museum includes about 1,500 instruments and features a complete 17th-century orchestra, a precious 1619 spinet-harpsichord (only two such instruments exist), a rare Chedeville bagpipe, and about 100 Indian instruments given to King Leopold II by the Rajah Sourindro Mohun Tagore. In addition to seeing the instruments, visitors may actually listen to them via infrared headphones, which play about 200 extracts ranging from ancient Greek times to the mid-20th century. In the basement, the Garden of Orpheus is set up for children to discover musical instruments. In addition, the museum's 200-seat concert hall hosts regular performances that feature harpsichords, virginals, and pianos from the collection. The tearoom and restaurant on the sixth floor offer panoramic views of Brussels. *R. Montagne de la Cour 2, tel. 02/545–0130. BF150/€3.70. Tues., Wed., and Fri. 9:30–5, Thurs. 9:30–8, weekends 10–5. Concerts Thursdays at 8.*

㉕ PALAIS DE JUSTICE. Many a nasty comment—"the ugliest building in Europe," for instance—has been made about Leopold II's giant late-19th-century Law Courts on the site of the old Gallows Hill. However, unlike the country's famously inept law enforcers, the pompous edifice actually strikes fear into the heart of the malefactor. Much of the Marolles district was pulled down to make way for the monstrosity, leaving thousands homeless. *Pl. Poelaert, tel. 02/508–6111. Entrance hall free. Weekdays 9–5.*

㉓ PARC DE BRUXELLES. This was once a game park, but in the late 18th century it was tamed into rigid symmetry and laid out in the design of Masonic symbols. The huge **Palais du Roi** occupies the entire south side of the park. It was built by Leopold II at the beginning of this century on a scale corresponding to his megalomaniacal ambitions. The present monarch, King Albert II, comes here for state occasions, although he lives at the more private Laeken Palace on the outskirts of Brussels. *Pl. des Palais, R. Royale, adjacent to Pl. Royale. Palais du Roi free. July 22–early Sept., Tues.–Sun. 10–4.*

★ **⑰ PLACE DU GRAND SABLON.** The Large Sand Place is where the people of Brussels come to see and be seen. Once, as the name implies, it was nothing more than a sandy hill. Today, it is an elegant square, surrounded by numerous restaurants, cafés, and antiques shops, some in intriguing alleys and arcades. Every Saturday and Sunday morning a lively antiques market of more than 100 stands takes over the upper end of the square. It's not for bargain hunters, however. Downhill from the square stands the **Eglise de la Chapelle**, dating from 1134. Inside, there's a memorial to Pieter Bruegel the Elder, who was married in this church and buried here just a few years later. At the eastern end of the square stands the **Eglise Notre-Dame du Sablon**, a Flamboyant-Gothic church founded in 1304 by the guild of crossbowmen (the original purpose of the square was crossbow practice) and rebuilt in the 15th century. It's one of Brussels's most beautiful churches, and at night the stained-glass windows are illuminated from within. *Intersection of R. de Rollebeek, R. Lebeau, R. de la Paille, R. Ste-Anne, R. Boedenbroeck, R. des Sablons, Petite Rue des Minimes, R. des Minimes, and R. Joseph Stevens.*

NEED A BREAK? **Wittamer,** the best of Brussels's many excellent pastry shops (Pl. du Grand Sablon 12, tel. 02/512–3742), has an attractive upstairs tearoom, which also serves breakfast and light lunches, featuring by Wittamer's unbeatable pastries.

⑱ PLACE DU PETIT SABLON. Opposite the Grand Sablon, this square is surrounded by a magnificent wrought-iron fence, topped by 48 small bronze statues representing the city's guilds. Inside the peaceful garden stands a double statue of the Flemish patriots Counts Egmont and Hoorn on their way to the Spaniards' scaffold in 1568.

㉔ PLACE LOUISE. There's a certain type of young Belgian matron—tall, blond, bejeweled, and freshly tanned whatever the season—whose natural urban habitat is around Place Louise. The most expensive shops are along Boulevard Waterloo. Prices are somewhat lower on the other side of the street, on Avenue de la Toison d'Or, which means the Golden Fleece. Additional shops and boutiques line both sides of Avenue Louise and the Galerie Louise, which burrows through the block to link Avenue de la Toison d'Or with Place Stéphanie. This is an area for browsing, window-shopping, movie-going, and café-sitting, but don't go expecting a bargain. *Av. Louise and Bd. de Waterloo.*

NEED A BREAK? **Nemrod** (Bd. de Waterloo 61, tel. 02/511–1127) is an expensive but handily placed café-pub garishly dressed up as a hunting lodge with a blazing fire. It's very popular for a shopping break or before a show.

★ ㉑ PLACE ROYALE. Although the Royal Square was built in the French style by Austrian overlords, it is distinctly Belgian. White and elegantly proportioned, it is the centerpiece of the Upper

Town, which became the center of power during the 18th century. The equestrian statue in its center, representing Godefroid de Bouillon, crusader and King of Jerusalem, is a romantic afterthought. The buildings are being restored one by one, leaving the facades intact. Place Royale was built on the ruins of the Palace of the Dukes of Brabant, which had burned down. The site has been excavated, and it is possible to see the underground digs and the main hall, Aula Magna, where Charles V was crowned Holy Roman Emperor in 1519 and where, 37 years later, he abdicated to retire to a monastery. The church on the square, **St-Jacques-sur-Coudenberg**, was originally designed to look like a Greek temple. After the French Revolution reached Belgium, it briefly served as a "Temple of Reason." The art nouveau building on the northwest corner is the former Old England department store, home of the Musée des Instruments de Musique.

On or near Place Royale are the neoclassical courtyard of the **Palace of Charles of Lorraine** (Coudenberg); the **Hôtel Ravenstein** (3 R. Ravenstein), built in the 15th century and the only surviving aristocratic house from that period; and the **Palais des Beaux-Arts** (23 R. Ravenstein), an art deco concert hall, designed in the 1920s by Victor Horta and remarkable more for the ingenuity with which he overcame its tricky location than for its aesthetic appeal.

OFF THE BEATEN PATH **ATOMIUM** – Built for the 1958 World's Fair, the model of an iron molecule enlarged 165 billion times is one of Brussels's landmarks. Take an express elevator to the top, 400 ft up, for panoramic views of Brussels. *Bd. du Centenaire, tel. 02/474–8904. BF200/€4.95. Apr.–Oct., daily 9–7; May–Sept., daily 10–5:30. Metro: Heysel.*

MINI-EUROPE – In a 5-acre park next to the Atomium stands an impressive collection of 1:25 scale models of more than 300 famous buildings from the 15 European Union countries. *Bd. du*

Centenaire 20, tel. 02/478–0550. BF420/€10.50. Daily 9:30–5 (July–Aug. until 7).

OCEADE – Attractions at this water park include water slides, a Jacuzzi, and a wave pool. Bruparck, near Atomium and next to Mini-Europe, tel. 02/478–4944. BF480/€11. 95. Tues.–Thurs. 10–6; Fri., weekends, and holidays 10–10.

MUSEUMS AND THE EU: CINQUANTENAIRE AND SCHUMAN

East of the center at the end of Rue de la Loi, Ronde-Point Robert Schuman is the focus of the buildings that house the European institutions. A number of vast museums flank Brussels's version of the Arc de Triomphe, known as Cinquantenaire, planned by Leopold II for the 50th anniversary of Belgian independence in 1880. Leopold's inability to coax funding from a reluctant government meant it was not completed until 25 years later.

Numbers in the text correspond to numbers in the margin and on the Cinquantenaire and Schuman map.

A Good Walk

Start at Rond-Point Schuman, where among the buildings of the **European Institutions** ㉘–㉚ you can see the Justus Lipsius Building, named for the Renaissance humanist and friend of Rubens and home to the secretive Council of Ministers. You can also see the Berlaymont, a star-shape building that is normally home to the European Commission. After having been closed due to an asbestos scare and spending eight years wrapped in plastic sheeting, it is due to reopen in October 2001 following a thorough environmental cleanup and complete rebuilding. Walk down Rue Archimede, with the Berlaymont building on your left, and continue until the street joins Square Ambiorix. The heavy presence of the European Union community is evident in the English- and Irish-style pubs. Turn left onto the square and continue in a counterclockwise direction on the square until it joins Avenue Palmerston. Take another left onto Palmerston until you reach Square Marie Louise, with its pond and false grotto—one of only three ponds left in Brussels from the approximately 60 that had existed in the 15th century. Continue on Palmerston. The Hotel Van Eetvelde at No. 44 was designed by art nouveau architect Victor Horta between 1895–1901 (here, *hotel* refers to a large, private house). After Palmerston rejoins Square Ambiorix, continue to No. 11, a curvaceous art nouveau treasure designed in 1900 by Gustave Strauven for painter Georges de St.-Cyr. Walk back across the square and turn left, then head right at Rue Michel Ange and continue until it ends at Avenue Cortenbergh. The Parc du Cinquantenaire is across the street. Continue east through the park until you reach the Cinquantenaire Musée, which houses the **Musée Royal de l'Armée et de l'Histoire Militaire** ③ and the **Musées Royaux d'Art et de l'Histoire** ㉜, and **Autoworld** ㉝. Walk down Avenue de Tervuren, a broad, straight road created by Leopold II at the end of the 19th century, to link the Cinquantenaire arch with Tervurn. When you reach Place Montgomery, take a 44 tram to Tervuren and the **Koninklijk Museum voor Midden Afrika/Musée Royal de l'Afrique Centrale.** ㉞

TIMING

From Ronde-Point Schuman, it's about 50 minutes to the Cinquantenaire Museum and Autoworld. To walk to Square Montgomery, allow around 30 minutes. The tram to Tervuren takes about 20 minutes.

Sights to See

㉝ **AUTOWORLD.** Here, under the high glass roof of the south hall in the Parc de Cinquantenaire, is arrayed one of the best collections of vintage cars in the world. More than 450 are in the stellar collection. *Parc du Cinquantenaire 11, tel. 02/736–4165. BF200/€4.95. Apr. 1–Sept. 30, daily 10–6; Oct. 1–Mar. 31, daily 10–5. Subway: Mérode.*

cinquantenaire

chausée de Louvain

blvd.Clovis

r. de Pavie

No.

rue du Marteau

Hotel Van Eetvelde

Sq. Marie Louis

ave. Palmerston

Sq. Amboirix

Parc de Bruxelles

rue de la Loi

rue Stevin

r. Archimide

r. de Lalaing

29

Berlaymont

boulevard du Régent

av. des Arts

rue du Commerce

rue Belliard

28

rond poi Schuma

pl. du Trône

rue de Trèves

r. de Pascal

ch. Etterbeek

Froissart

Sq. de Meeus

r. de Parnasse

rue Wiertz

30

Parc Leopold

rue du Trone

ave. de Maelbeek

r.

chausée de Wavre

Gare du Quartier Léopold

chausée de Wavre

r.Gen. Leh

0 — 400 yards
0 — 400 meters

Autoworld, 33

European Commission, 28

European Council of Ministers, 29

European Parliament, 30

Koninklijk Museum voor Midden Afrika, 34

Musée Royal de L'Armee et de L'Histoire Millitaire, 31

Musées Royaux d'Art et de l'Histoire, 32

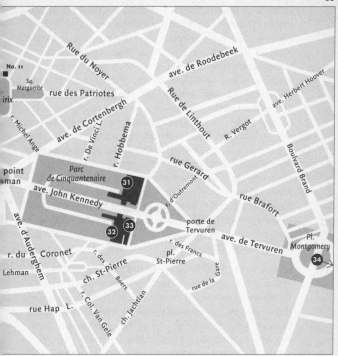

EUROPEAN INSTITUTIONS. The European Commission and related institutions have had a significant impact on Brussels. Entire neighborhoods east of the center have been razed to make room for steel-and-glass buildings. What remains of the old blocks has also seen an influx of ethnic restaurants catering to the tastes of lower-level Eurocrats; the grandees eat in splendid isolation in their own dining rooms. The landmark, star-shape Berlaymont building was closed in 1991 for asbestos removal. Following a full environmental cleanup and restoration it is to reopen in October 2001. During the work, the **European Commission** (R. de Trèves 120) and the **European Council of Ministers** (R. de la Loi 170) are occupying temporary headquarters. The controversial **European Parliament** building (R. Wiertz 43)—France still insists on regular Parliament meetings in Strasbourg—is named Les Caprices des Dieux, or Folly of the Gods. Its central element, a rounded glass summit, looms behind the Gare de Luxembourg. *Rond-Point R. Schuman. Subway: from Ste-Cathérine via De Brouckère to Schuman.*

MUSÉE DES TRANSPORTS URBAINS BRUXELLOIS. The Museum of Brussels Urban Transport houses historic trams and buses—rides are offered as well. The museum also organizes tourist visits on historic trams on Sunday mornings from April to October for BF400/€9.95, including a beverage, or for BF700/€17.50 including a meal. *Avenue du Tervuren 364b, tel. 02/515–3108. BF50/€1.25 or BF150/€3.70 including a tram ride. Apr.–Oct., weekends 1:30–7.*

KONINKLIJK MUSEUM VOOR MIDDEN AFRIKA/MUSÉE ROYAL DE L'AFRIQUE CENTRALE. The Africa Museum is part of King Leopold II's legacy to Belgium, an incredible collection of 250,000 objects, including masks, sculpture, and memorabilia of the journeys of the explorers of Africa. The museum stands in the middle of a beautifully landscaped park. *Leuvensesteenweg 13, tel. 02/767–5401. BF50/€1.25. Tues.–Fri. 10–5, weekends 10–6. Subway: to Pl. Montgomery, then Tram 44 to Tervuren.*

③① **MUSÉE ROYAL DE L'ARMÉE ET DE L'HISTOIRE MILITAIRE.** The highlight of this vast collection of the Royal Museum of Arms and Military History, part of the Cinquantenaire Museum, is the hall filled with 130 aircraft from World War I to the Gulf War. *Parc du Cinquantenaire 3, tel. 02/733–4493. Free. Tues.–Sun. 9–noon and 1–4:30.*

★ **③②** **MUSÉES ROYAUX D'ART ET DE L'HISTOIRE.** The 140 rooms at the Royal Museums of Art and History contain important antiquities and ethnographic collections. The most significant sections are devoted to Belgian archaeology and to the immense tapestries for which Brussels once was famous. Renovations in the late 1990s have brought to the museum a new treasure room, plenty of temporary exhibitions, and a more dynamic approach, as well as a new name, joining it with the Musée Royal de l'Armée et de l'Histoire Militaire as the Cinquantenaire Museum. *Parc du Cinquantenaire 10, tel. 02/ 741–7211. BF100. Tues.–Fri. 9:30–5, weekends 10–5.*

EAST OF THE CENTER
A Good Walk

Begin at the **Musée des Sciences Naturelles** on Rue Vautier, where the hulking sculpture of a dinosaur outside is a precursor to the museum's collection. Continue on Rue Vautier to the **Musée Wiertz,** housed in the studio of 19th-century classical artist Antoine Wiertz. Turn right from Rue Vautier onto Rue Wiertz, taking you through the **European Parliament,** a 13-story behemoth. From Rue Wiertz walk through **Parc Leopold** to enjoy a respite from the city. Turn right onto Rue Beillard and then left on Rue Froissart to head to the Schuman metro station. From Schuman it's a short metro ride to the Arts-Loi station, handy for a visit to the **Musée Charlier,** the former residence of sculptor Guillaume Charlier.

TIMING

It's about a 10-minute walk from the Natural Science Museum to the European Parliament. Allow another 20 minutes to walk to the Schuman metro station and another five minutes on the Metro to Arts-Loi. Including museums, the visit should take about an hour and a half.

Sights to See

MUSÉE CHARLIER. The former home of 19th-century sculptor Guillaume Charlier is now a museum housing both his own work and his collection of paintings, sculpture, tapestry, and furniture from the 15th through 19th centuries. *Av. des Arts 16, tel. 02/218–5382. BF200/€4.95. Tues.–Sun. 10–6.*

MUSÉE DES SCIENCES NATUREL. The highlights of the Natural Sciences Museum are the skeletons of 14 iguanodons found in 1878 in the coal mines of Bernissart—these are believed to be about 120 million years old. There are also displays on mammals, insects, and tropical shells, as well as a whale gallery. *R. Vautier 29, tel. 02/627–4211. BF120/€2.95. Tues.–Sat. 9:30–4:45, Sun. 9:30–6.*

MUSÉE WIERTZ. Antoine Wiertz was an early 19th-century artist who once won the Grand Prize of Rome for a classical painting. He later adopted the style of Flemish grand master Pieter Paul Rubens, but failing to find success turned to portrait painting. The Belgian government in 1850 gave him a studio in exchange for some of his works, and he later lived in an adjoining house. The museum is housed in the studio. *R. Vautier 62, tel. 02/648–1718. Free. Tues.–Fri. 10–noon and 1–5, every other weekend 10–noon and 1–5.*

WEST OF THE CENTER
A Good Walk

Start with a walk westward from Boulevard du Midi to the **Gueuze Museum.** Take Rue Crickx or Rue Brogniez to Rue Gheude, then walk north to the end of the street. Or, take a short detour before heading to the Gueuze by turning right onto Avenue de Stalingrad to visit the **Musée Juif de Belgique.** From the Gueuze, take a taxi or the 47 tram on Chaussée de Mons to

Place de la Vaillance. Rue du Chapître, with the **Anderlecht Béguinage** and the **Maison d'Erasme,** is on your right.

TIMING
It's a 5- to 10-minute walk from the Kermesse to Gueuze. The tram ride takes about 10 minutes.

Sights to See

ANDERLECHT BÉGUINAGE. The Béguines, lay sisters and mostly widows of Crusaders, lived here in a collection of small houses, built between 1252 and the 17th century, grouped around a garden. Now it's open to the public, sharing a common administrative office with the Erasmushuis (☞ Maison d'Erasme, *below*). *R. du Chapître 8.*

GUEUZE MUSEUM. At this living museum of the noble art of brewing you can see Lambic being produced the old way, and also enjoy a tasting. The quintessential Brussels beer, created through spontaneous fermentation, is brewed nowhere else and is the basic ingredient in other popular Belgian beers, such as Gueuze, cherry-flavored Kriek, and raspberry-flavored Framboise. Sadly, many of the commercially brewed Lambics bear scant resemblance to the real thing. *R. Gheude 56, tel. 02/521–4928. BF100/€2.50. Weekdays 8:30–5, Sat. 10–5 (mid-Oct.–May, until 6). Metro: Gare du Midi.*

MUSÉE JUIF DE BELGIQUE. The Jewish Museum of Belgium's houses a collection of religious objects dating from the 16th century, as well as documents and books that illustrate traditional Jewish life. In addition to objects that illustrate Jewish customs throughout Europe are a number of pieces, including textiles and silver, made in Belgium. *Avenue de Stalingrad, tel. 02/512–1963. BF100/€2.50. Mon.–Thurs. noon–5, Sun. 10–1. Metro: Lemonnier.*

MAISON D'ERASME/ERASMUSHUIS. In the middle of a commonplace neighborhood in the commune of Anderlecht stands the remarkable redbrick Erasmus House, which has been restored to its condition in 1521, the year the great humanist came to Brussels for the fresh air. First editions of In Praise of Folly, and other books by Erasmus can be inspected, and there are some extraordinary works of art: prints by Albrecht Dürer and oils by Holbein and Hieronymus Bosch. Erasmus was out of tune with the ecclesiastical authorities of his day, and some of the pages on view show where the censors stepped in to protect the faithful. R. du Chapître 31, tel. 02/521–1383. BF50. Wed.–Thurs. and Sat.–Mon. 10–noon and 2–5. Subway: Ste-Catherine to St-Guidon station in Anderlecht commune.

SOUTH OF THE CENTER: ART DECO AND ART NOUVEAU
A Good Walk

Start at the art deco **Musée David-et-Alice-Van-Buuren** ㉟, off the commune of Uccle's Rond-Point Churchill; then return to the circle and head left along the affluent Avenue Winston Churchill until you reach Place Vanderkindere. From here, turn right and head down Avenue Brugmann, past a remarkable assortment of art nouveau houses. Look particularly for Brunfaut's Hôtel Hannon, at the intersection of Brugmann and Avenue de la Jonction, and the charming redbrick Les Hiboux next door. Cross Chaussée de Waterloo and head up Chaussée de Charleroi, then head right onto Rue Américaine to the **Musée Horta** ㊱. Continue on Rue Américaine, then turn left on Rue du Page, crossing Place du Chatelain and turning left on Rue Simonis. Take a right on Rue du Bailli, then turn left onto Rue du Livourne. Turn right on Rue Paul-Émile Janson, stopping at No. 6 to see the Tassel house, also designed by Victor Horta. At Avenue Louise turn right, keeping your eye open for the Hotel Solvay at No. 224, which is generally considered Horta's finest work. Continue on Avenue Louise to the roundabout and turn left onto Rue de la Monastère. Pick up Avenue Bernier, cross Avenue de la Hippodrome, and you're on Rue du Bourmestre.

The **Musée des Enfants** ㊲ is on the left. If you like, circle back east past the Abbaye de la Czmbre to the **Musée Constantin Neunier** ㊳.

TIMING

Allow two or three hours for this walk, including time in the museums, the 20-minute walk from the Van Buuren to the Horta Museum, and the 15 or so minutes to the Musée des Enfants.

Sights to See

㊳ **MUSÉE CONSTANTIN MEUNIER.** Nineteenth-century painter and sculptor Constantin Meunier made his mark capturing the hardships of Belgian workers in a distinctive and realistic style. Both his paintings and sculptures are displayed in his former house and studio. *Rue de l'Abbaye 59, tel. 02/648–4449. Free. Tues.–Sun. 10–noon and 1–5.*

㉟ **MUSÉE DAVID-ET-ALICE-VAN-BUUREN.** A perfect art deco interior from the 1930s is preserved in this museum. The made-to-order carpets and furnishings are supplemented by paintings by the Van Buurens, as well as Old Masters including a Bruegel, *Fall of Icarus*, one of the three versions he painted. The house is surrounded by lush formal gardens. *Av. Leo Errera 41, tel. 02/343–4851. BF300/€7.40, BF500/€12.40 for house and gardens. Sun. 1–6, Mon. 2–6, Tues.–Sat. by appointment for groups of up to 20. Trams 23 and 90.*

㊲ **MUSÉE DES ENFANTS** (Children's Museum). At this museum for 2- to 12-year-olds, the purpose may be educational—learning to handle objects and emotions—but the results are fun. Kids get to plunge their arms into sticky goo, dress up in eccentric costumes, walk through a hall of mirrors, crawl through tunnels, and take photographs with an oversize camera. *R. du Bourgmestre 15, tel. 02/640–0107. BF200. Sept.–July, Wed. and weekends 2:30–5. Trams 93 and 94.*

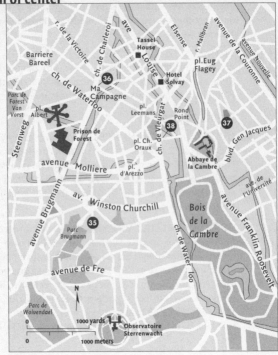

Musée Constantin
Meunier, 38

Musée
David-et-Alice-
Van-Buuren, 35

Musée des
Enfants, 37

Musée
Horta, 36

★ ③⑥ **MUSÉE HORTA.** The house where Victor Horta (1861–1947), the creator of art nouveau, lived and worked until 1919 is the best place to see his joyful interiors and furniture. Horta's genius lay in his ability to create a sense of opulence, light, and spaciousness where little light or space existed. Lamps hang from the ceilings like tendrils, and mirrored skylights evoke giant butterflies with multicolor wings of glass and steel. For examples of how Horta and his colleagues transformed the face of Brussels in little more than 10 years, ride down Avenue Louise to Vleurgat and walk along Rue Vilain XIIII to the area surrounding the **ponds of Ixelles**. R. Américaine 25, tel. 02/543–0490. BF150/€3.70 (weekends BF200/€4.95). Tues.–Sun. 2–5:30. To house: Tram 91 or 92 to Ma Campagne. To Ixelles: Tram 93 or 94.

In This Chapter

Updated by Katharine Mill

eating out

THE STAR-STUDDED BRUSSELS restaurant scene is a boon to visitors and natives alike. Some suggest that the European Commission chose Brussels for its headquarters because of the excellence of its restaurants. Although this may not be wholly true, the top Brussels restaurants rival the best Parisian restaurants; so, alas, do the prices. Most Belgians, however, value haute cuisine as a work of art and are prepared to part with a substantial sum for a special occasion.

A number of neighborhood restaurants have risen to the challenge of making dining out affordable. The choice of dishes may be more limited, and the ingredients less costly, but an animated ambience more than makes up for it. The tab is likely to be a quarter of what a dinner would cost you in one of the grand restaurants, and the uniformly high quality puts Paris to shame. The city is also richly endowed with good and mostly inexpensive Vietnamese, Italian, and Portuguese restaurants.

You can reduce the check almost by half by choosing a set menu. Fixed-price luncheon menus are often an especially good bargain. Menus and prices are always posted outside restaurants. Don't feel that you're under an obligation to eat a three-course meal; many people order just a main course. If you don't want two full restaurant meals a day, there are plenty of snack bars for a light midday meal, and most cafés serve sandwiches and light hot meals both noon and night.

CATEGORY	COST*
$$$$	over BF3,500/€85
$$$	BF2,500–BF3,500/€60–€85
$$	BF1,500–BF2,500/€35–€60
$	under BF1,500/€.35

*per person for a three-course meal, including service, taxes, but not beverages

LOWER TOWN

$$$$ COMME CHEZ SOI. ★ Pierre Wynants, the perfectionist owner-chef, has decorated his bistro-size restaurant in sumptuous art nouveau style. The superb cuisine, excellent wines, and attentive service complement the warm decor. Wynants is ceaselessly inventive, and earlier creations are quickly relegated to the back page of the menu. One all-time favorite, fillet of sole with a white wine mousseline and shrimp, is, however, always available. One minus: ventilation is poor and it can get very smoky. Pl. Rouppe 23, tel. 02/512–2921. Reservations essential. Jacket and tie. AE, DC, MC, V. Closed Sun.–Mon., July, Dec. 25–Jan. 1.

$$$$ MAISON DU CYGNE. With decor to match its classic cuisine, this restaurant is set in a 17th-century guildhall on the Grand'Place. It's the place to go for power dining. The paneled walls of the formal dining room upstairs are hung with Old Masters, and a small room on the mezzanine contains two priceless Bruegels. Service is flawless in the grand manner of old. Typical French-Belgian dishes include *cocotte d'écrévisses et petits gris de Namur* (shrimp and crayfish), and *agneau pavillac à Cygne* (lamb). R. Charles Buyls 2, tel. 02/511–8244. Reservations essential. Jacket and tie. AE, DC, MC, V. No lunch Sat. Closed Sun. and 3 wks in Aug.

$$$ ALBAN CHAMBON. The eatery of the splendid Belle Epoque Mètropole Hotel lives up to the style of its surroundings. Named after its architect, the gastronomic restaurant sparkles with light from chandeliers reflected in the mirrors all round, while piano music filters in from the bar next door. The cuisine, wine list, and service are all one would expect in such grandiose surroundings: diners can munch on large raviolis of langoustine with wild mushrooms and white sauce, or fried fillet of lamb with vegetable and mint tabbouleh and new potatoes. *Mètropole Hotel, Place de Broucère, tel. 02/217–2300. AE, DC, MC, V. Closed weekends.*

$$$ L'EPICERIE. Highly acclaimed young chef David Martin blends the traditional with the exotic in this, the restaurant of the Meridien Hotel, opposite the Gare Centrale. The results are daring adventures in international flavors. In an elegant, Mediterranean-style setting, diners feast on sea bass with cocoa and thyme-flavored caramelized salsify; or hare in a sauce of dates, chestnuts, and oranges. On Sundays, a self-service brunch is served in place of the usual menu. A pianist tinkles away in the background every evening except Sunday. *Meridien Hotel, Carrefour de l'Europe 3, tel. 02/548–4716. AE, DC, MC, V. No lunch Sat.*

$$$ OGENBLIK. This small, split-level restaurant, in a side alley off
★ the Galeries St-Hubert, has all the trappings of an old-time bistro: green-shaded lamps over marble-top tables, sawdust on the floor, and laid-back waiters. There's nothing casual about the French-style cuisine, however: grilled sweetbreads with courgette gratin, millefeuille of lobster and salmon with a coulis of langoustines, saddle of lamb with spring vegetables and potato gratin. The selection of Beaujolais is particularly good. *Galerie des Princes 1, tel. 02/511–6151. AE, DC, MC, V. Open until midnight. Closed Sun.*

$$$ SEA GRILL. Dashing superstar chef Yves Mattagne presides in the
★ kitchen of this, arguably the best seafood place in town and one of the restaurants in the Radisson SAS Hotel. Gastronomes rub shoulders here with tycoons and aristocrats, as they tuck into king crab from the Barents Sea, Brittany lobster in lobster press sauce, and line-caught sea bass prepared in crusted sea salt. Inevitably, because of its hotel situation, the restaurant has a rather corporate feel, but it is spacious and elegant, and service is impeccable.

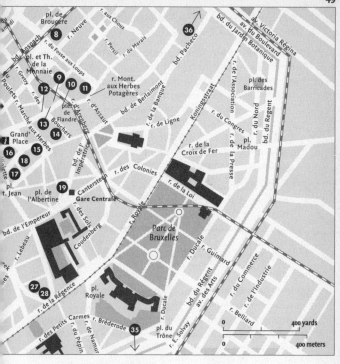

L'Ecailler du
Palais Royal, 28

L'Epicerie, 19

Le Saint-
Boniface, 35

Les Capucines, 32

Les Petits
Oignons, 25

L'Idiot du
Village, 26

Maison du
Cygne, 16

Ogenblik, 10

Sea Grill, 11

Strofilia, 1

Taverne du
Passage, 14

't Kelderke, 15

Vincent, 9

Radisson SAS Hotel, R. du Fossè aux loups, tel. 02/227–3120. AE, DC, MC, V. No lunch Sat. Closed Sun.

$$ AUX ARMES DE BRUXELLES. Hidden among the tourist traps of the Ilôt Sacré, this child-friendly restaurant attracts a largely local clientele with its slightly tarnished middle-class elegance and its Belgian classics: turbot waterzooi, eels in green sauce, a variety of steaks, mussels prepared every which way, and frites (french fries), which the Belgians believe, with some justification, they prepare better than anyone else. The place is cheerful and light, and service is friendly if frequently overstretched. R. des Bouchers 13, tel. 02/511–5550. AE, DC, MC, V. Closed Mon.

$$ BIJ DEN BOER. This old-fashioned Brussels bistro with wooden benches and mirrors does good, honest fish and seafood in an informal atmosphere near the old fish market. It serves classic Belgian seafood dishes, such as grey shrimp croquettes, eels in green sauce, and mussels, as well as the southern French bouillabaisse. Quai aux Briques 60, tel. 02/512–6122. AE, DC, MC, V. Closed Sun.

$$ IN 'T SPINNEKOPKE. This is where true Brussels cooking has survived and continues to flourish. The low ceilings and benches around the walls remain from its days as a coach inn during the 18th century. You can choose from among 100 artisanal beers, and many dishes are made with beer. Pl. du Jardin aux Fleurs 1, tel. 02/511–8695. AE, DC, MC, V. No lunch Sat. Closed Sun.

$$ JACQUES. Quality and simplicity are the watchwords in this busy fish restaurant, which serves its speciality unadorned, with just boiled potatoes or frites and a simple green salad. Eels in green sauce, tomatoes stuffed with tiny grey shrimps, and scampi with garlic are typical of the Belgian specialities dished up in a bistro setting. Lobster must be ordered in advance and sauces are available as extras. A note of warning: it's noisy and smoky, and service is on the surly side. Quai aux Briques 44, tel. 02/513–2762. No credit cards. Closed Sun. and July.

$$ LA MANUFACTURE. A former leather goods factory (for Belgian handbag brand Delvaux) converted into a restaurant of modern, industrial design, this place attracts a fashionable crowd that spills over into a quiet, sheltered courtyard. The cuisine mixes Mediterranean and Asian influences and the wine list is good, but people mostly come here for the superb setting. *R. Notre Dame du Sommeil, tel. 02/502–2525. AE, DC, MC, V. No lunch Sat. Closed Sun.*

$$ LA ROUE D'OR. This art nouveau brasserie has bright orange and yellow murals that pay humorous homage to Surrealist René Magritte. Bowler-hatted gentlemen ascend serenely to the ceiling, a blue sky inhabited by tropical birds. The good cuisine includes traditional Belgian fare—a generous fish waterzooi and homemade frites—as well as such staples of the French brasserie repertory as lamb's tongue vinaigrette with shallots, veal kidneys with tarragon and watercress cream, and foie gras. *R. des Chapeliers 26, tel. 02/514–2554. AE, DC, MC, V. Closed approximately July 15–Aug. 15.*

$$ TAVERNE DU PASSAGE. This art deco brasserie in the famous shopping arcade has been here since 1928 and remains a classic of its kind, serving chicken waterzooi, sauerkraut, and lobster from noon to midnight nonstop. Most fun of all, however, are the roasts, which are carved in front of you. The waiters are multilingual and jolly and the wine list is exceptional—not surprising in a restaurant owned by the president of the Belgian guild of wine waiters. Reserve a table outside if you like to watch the world go by. *Gal. de la Reine 30, tel. 02/512–3731. AE, DC, MC, V. Closed Wed. and Thurs. in June and July.*

$$ VINCENT. In a town where most of the fashionable places now concentrate on seafood, Vincent unapologetically remains a red-meat stronghold. Sides of beef and big slabs of butter in the window announce what awaits you. You pass through the kitchen on your way to the dining room, which is decorated with hand-painted tiles. *R. des Dominicains 8–10, tel. 02/511–2303. AE, DC, MC, V. Closed 1st two wks Aug.*

52

$ BONSOIR CLARA. On downtown's trendy Rue Dansaert, this is the jewel in the crown of young restaurateur Frédéric Nicolay, who runs half a dozen fashionable cafés and eateries in the capital, including the Kasbah next door. An upbeat, refined brasserie serving excellent caramelized duck as well as fish and red-meat dishes, it's best-known for eye-catching decor, especially a back wall entirely composed of large colored squares, as if you were in a Rubik's Cube factory. *R. Dansaert 22, tel. 02/502–0990. AE, MC, V. No lunch weekends.*

$ CHEZ JEAN. Jean Cambien runs a reliable, unpretentious
★ restaurant, unchanged since 1931. Oak benches sit against the walls, which are backed by mirrors upon which the dishes of the day are written in whitewash. Waitresses in black and white serve poached cod, mussels cooked in white wine, chicken waterzooi (with free seconds and thirds), chicken in kriek (cherry-flavored lambic beer) with cherries, and other quintessentially Belgian fare. *R. des Chapeliers 6, tel. 02/511–9815. AE, DC, MC, V. Closed Sun. and June.*

$ CHEZ LÉON DE BRUXELLES. More than a century old, this cheerful
★ restaurant has over the years expanded into a row of eight old houses, while its franchises can now be found across Belgium and even in Paris. Heaped plates of mussels and other Belgian specialties, such as eels in a green sauce and fish soup, are continually served, accompanied by arguably the best french fries in town. *R. des Bouchers 18, tel. 02/511–1415. AE, DC, MC, V.*

$ FALSTAFF. After a surprise bankruptcy that kept it closed for
★ several months in 1999, this huge Brussels tavern with the wonderful art nouveau interior was bought and renovated by a Paris investor. Fears that it would lose its character seem unfounded, however; apart from an extensive menu of cocktails and some Cuban sounds, it still dishes up the straightforward Belgian cuisine that makes it popular with everyone from students to pensioners. Customers are welcome well into the early hours (5 AM on weekends). The Latin-flavored Montecristo Café next door

is owned by the same group and gets louder and fuller the later it gets. *R. Henri Maus 19, tel. 02/511–9877. AE, DC, MC, V.*

$ STROFILIA. Set in a restored 17th-century warehouse with exposed brick walls and a magnificent vaulted wine cellar, this restaurant does a good selection of hot and cold meze to mix and match, as well as salads for vegetarians. Eggplant purée with pine nuts and minced lamb kebabs are among the choices. It's open until 1 AM on Friday and Saturday. *R. du Marché aux Porcs 11–13, tel. 02/512–3293. AE, DC, MC, V. No lunch. Closed Sun.*

$ 'T KELDERKE. This beautiful, 17th-century vaulted cellar restaurant features traditional Belgian cuisine served at plain wooden tables. Portions are generous and mussels are the house specialty. It's a popular place with locals, open from noon to 2 AM; even the house cat is friendly. Beware of the low door frame when entering. *Grand'Place 15, tel. 02/513–7344. AE, DC, MC, V.*

SOUTH OF CENTER

$$$$ LA TRUFFE NOIRE. ★ Luigi Ciciriello's "Black Truffle" attracts a sophisticated clientele with its modern design, well-spaced tables, and cuisine that draws on classic Italian and modern French cooking. Carpaccio is prepared at the table and served with long strips of truffle and Parmesan. Entrées may include Vendé pigeon with truffles, steamed John Dory with truffles and leeks, and leg of Pauillac lamb in pie crust. The restaurant also has a garden. *Bd. de la Cambre 12, tel. 02/640–4422. Reservations essential. Jacket and tie. AE, DC, MC, V. No lunch Sat. Closed Sun., Jan. 1–10, last wk July, 1st 2 wks Aug.*

$$$$ VILLA LORRAINE. Generations of American business travelers have been introduced to the three-hour Belgian lunch at the opulent Villa, on the edge of the Bois de la Cambre. The green terrace room is light, elegant, and airy, and there's alfresco dining under the spreading chestnut tree. Feast on emincé of lobster with tomatoes, mozzarella and pesto, fried sweetbreads *forestière*

metropolitan brussels dining

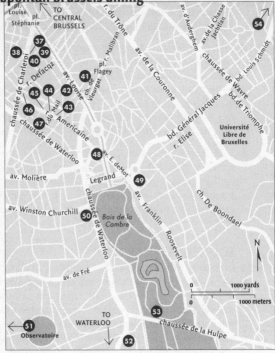

(garnished with morels, bacon, and sautéed potatoes), or quails and duckling with peaches and green pepper. *Chaussée de la Hulpe 28, tel. 02/374–3163. Jacket and tie. AE, DC, MC, V. Closed Sun. and 1st 3 wks July.*

$$$ LA PORTE DES INDES. This is the city's foremost Indian restaurant—the creation of Karl Steppe, a Belgian antiques dealer turned restaurateur, who also owns the global Blue Elephant chain. The gracious staff wears traditional Indian attire. The plant-filled lobby, wood carvings, and rich red and mauve decor provide a luxuriant backdrop. The cuisine ranges from a mild pilaf to a spicy vindaloo. The "brass tray" offers an assortment of specialties. A vegetarian menu is also available. *Av. Louise 455, tel. 02/647–8651. AE, DC, MC, V. No lunch Sun.*

$$ BISTRO DU MAIL. By no means a bistro in the fast-food sense, this popular Ixelles restaurant does sophisticated modern French food: roast Landaise chicken with rosemary and olives, and poached foie gras with chanterelle mushrooms and baby leeks are two of the succulent choices. The elegant setting has trendy terra-cotta walls and jazz playing in the background. *R. du Mail 81, tel. 02/539–0697. AE, DC, MC, V. No lunch Sat. Closed Sun.*

$$ BLUE ELEPHANT. In the suburb of Uccle, this excellent Thai restaurant is owned by Karl Steppe, the antiquarian behind the city's top Indian restaurant, La Porte des Indes. Opened in 1975, this is the cornerstone of the Blue Elephant empire, which now extends to London, Paris, Copenhagen, New Delhi, Dubai, and Beirut. Inside, it's like a tropical garden scattered with southeast Asian antiques; daylight floods in from above and filters through the splendid greenery and exotic flower arrangements. The food is just as impressive: curries seasoned with lemongrass, coconut milk, and aromatic spices. The set lunch is a good value. *Ch. de Waterloo 1120, tel. 02/374–4962. AE, DC, MC, V. No lunch Sat.*

$$ BRASSERIES GEORGES. This brash, hugely successful brasserie
★ was the first in Brussels and is still the best. Efficient service and

quality food is guaranteed. Past the splendid display of shellfish at the entrance, an art deco interior with a tile floor and potted palms awaits. Fast, efficient service is the hallmark of waitresses in black-and-white uniforms. Traditional dishes include sauerkraut, poached cod, and potted duck, while among the more adventurous dishes are salmon tartare and swordfish chop with a light chicory curry. Shellfish is the speciality. Twenty-five different wines are sold by the glass. *Av. Winston Churchill 259, tel. 02/347–2100. AE, DC, MC, V.*

$$ LE FILS DE JULES. Vivid, colorful Basque cuisine from southwest France is served with wines to match within the candlelit, art deco–inspired setting. A well-heeled, local crowd flocks here to sup on warm foie gras with grapes, and tartare of tuna with tapenade. *R. du Page 37, tel. 02/534–0057. AE, DC, MC, V. No lunch weekends.*

$$ LE FORCADO. Not a knob of butter can be found in this Portuguese restaurant where olive oil reigns supreme. Decorated in beautiful, blue and white antique tiles, it's the stylish eatery of choice for the capital's large Portuguese community. The speciality is the national dish of *baccalhau* (salt cod), which can be prepared every which way: try it simply grilled with garlic and olive oil. For a final treat, sample the pastries—made on the premises—with eggs, almonds, and oranges. The patisserie just round the corner on R. Américaine sells these, too. *Ch. de Charleroi 192, tel. 02/537–9220. AE, DC, MC, V. Closed Sun., Mon., and Aug.*

$$ MAJESTIC. Grandiose, plush decor makes this town house restaurant and bar a fashionable hangout for an upwardly mobile crowd. Even the bathroom taps are a design statement. The cuisine, French with Asian influences, is equally trendy; however, it doesn't compromise on quality as might be expected. Baby lobster roasted in sauternes and flavored with curry, and duck's liver with roast figs in port are two of the dishes on offer. *R. du Magistrat 33, tel. 02/639–1330. AE, MC, V. No lunch.*

When it Comes to Getting Local Currency at an ATM, Same Thing.

Whether you're in Yosemite or Yemen, using your Visa® card or ATM card with the PLUS symbol is the easiest and most convenient way to get local currency. For example, let's say you're in France. When you make a withdrawal, using your secured PIN, it's dispensed in francs, but is debited from your account in U.S. dollars. This makes it easy to take advantage of favorable exchange rates. And if you need help finding one of Visa's 627,000 ATMs in 127 countries worldwide, visit **visa.com/pd/atm**. We'll make finding an ATM as easy as finding the Eiffel Tower, the Pyramids or even the Grand Canyon.

It's Everywhere You Want To Be.®

SEE THE WORLD IN FULL COLOR

Fodor's Exploring Guides bring all the great sights vividly to life with hundreds of photographs, fascinating historical background, and colorful anecdotes. Detailed maps and practical information keep you headed in the right direction.

Pair a Fodor's Exploring Guide with your trusted Fodor's Pocket Guide for a complete planning package.

Fodor's EXPLORING GUIDES

At bookstores everywhere.

$$ LE PAIN ET LE VIN. Good taste reigns supreme in this suburban
★ temple to quality food and drink. Reopened in 2000, renovations
added a contemporary, minimalist decor of dazzling white, with
dark wood seating. The restaurant is co-owned by acclaimed
sommelier Eric Boschman; hence, the cellar is excellent, and
wines can be ordered by the glass to accompany different courses
of the pared-down cuisine. The large, paved garden surrounded
by greenery is a plus in fine weather. *Ch. d'Alsemberg 812A, tel. 02/
332–3774. AE, MC, V. No lunch Sat. Closed Sun.*

$$ LA QUINCAILLERIE. The name means "The Hardware Store,"
and that's precisely what this place used to be. It still looks the
part, except now there are tables perched on the narrow balcony,
and there's an oyster bar downstairs. It attracts a youngish,
upwardly mobile clientele and offers good deals on business
lunches. The menu consists mostly of brasserie grub, such as
baked ham knuckle, but it's enlivened by such selections as
honey-baked Barbary duck with lime, and a glorious seafood
platter. Regional and international specialties are often featured.
R. du Page 45, tel. 02/538–2553. AE, DC, MC, V. No lunch weekends.

$$ THOUMIEUX. One of the best-known brasseries in Paris brought
a flavor of the French capital to a corner site in Ixelles, down the
road from the Horta Museum. The traditional setting includes
mirrors, cushioned benches, crisp white tablecloths, and waiters
in long, starched aprons. On the menu are such French regional
specialities as cassoulet, a bean and meat stew from the southwest,
as well as typical brasserie staples: a seafood platter with lobster,
and sweetbreads with egg, shallot, and herb dressing. *R. Américaine
124, tel. 02/538–9909. AE, MC, V. Closed Sun.*

$ KUSHI-TEI OF TOKYO. This restaurant offers an authentic Japanese
experience that is sushi-free. It specializes in *kushiyaki* (wooden
skewers of meat and vegetables grilled over charcoal), including
chicken teriyaki. The chef works in sight of diners behind a counter.
Wine, sake, and Japanese beer are available. *R. Lesbroussart 118,
tel. 02/646–4815. AE, DC, MC, V. No lunch Sat. Closed Sun.*

UPPER TOWN

$$$$ L'ECAILLER DU PALAIS ROYAL. This excellent seafood-only restaurant, just off the Grand Sablon, feels like a comfortable club; many of the clients seem to have known one another and the staff for years. The menu changes twice annually, but such delicacies as risotto of prawns in champagne, lobster ravioli, and top-quality turbot were among the recent choices. *R. Bodenbroek 18, tel. 02/512–8751. Reservations essential. Jacket and tie. AE, DC, MC, V. Closed Sun., Easter wk, Aug.*

$$$ LES CAPUCINES. This pleasant restaurant stands out amid the mediocre eateries in the Place Louise shopping area. The dining room is inviting, decorated in shades of green, with huge flower arrangements. Chef Pierre Burtonboy prepares such delicate dishes as grilled fillet of sea bream, set on a bed of shredded leek and dressed with nut oil; lamb interleaved with goose liver, rolled and encased in pastry, with rosemary and thinly sliced potatoes; bitter chocolate mousse with crème anglaise; and iced peach soup with mint. *R. Jourdan 22, tel. 02/538–6924. AE, DC, MC, V. No dinner Mon. Closed Sun., Easter, and 2nd ½ of Aug.*

$$$ CASTELLO BANFI. On the Grand Sablon in beige-and-brown postmodern surroundings, you can enjoy classic French and Italian dishes with added refinements, such as toasted pine nuts with pesto. There's excellent carpaccio with Parmesan and celery, red mullet with ratatouille, and unbelievable mascarpone. The quality of the ingredients (sublime olive oil, milk-fed veal imported from France) is very high. The wine list is strong on fine Chianti aged in wood. *R. Bodenbroek 12, tel. 02/512–8794. Jacket and tie. AE, DC, MC, V. No dinner Sun. Closed Mon., Easter wk, Christmas wk, and last 3 wks Aug.*

$$$ INADA. This restaurant on a residential street near the Porte de Hal does exceptional French cuisine courtesy of Japanese chef and owner, Saburo Inada, who reportedly gets his poultry from the same supplier as French President Jacques Chirac. The approach is low-key, but the linen-covered tables are well-spaced and the food and wine are excellent. The dishes incorporate subtle Asian references, such as the young caramelized pigeon in an Oriental sauce, and Japanese-style grilled-eel salad. *R. de la Source 73, tel. 02/538–0113. AE, MC, V. No lunch Sat. Closed Sun., Mon., last 2 wks July, and 1st wk Aug.*

$$ AU STEKERLAPATTE. In the shadow of the Palais de Justice, this efficient, down-to-earth bistro serves Belgian specialties that include cassoulet, sauerkraut, grilled pig's trotters, spare ribs, and black pudding with caramelized apples. *R. des Prêtres 4, tel. 02/512–8681. MC, V. No lunch. Closed Mon.*

$$ AU VIEUX SAINT MARTIN. Even when neighboring restaurants on
★ Grand Sablon are empty, this one is full. A rack of glossy magazines is a thoughtful touch for lone diners, and you're equally welcome whether you order a cup of coffee or a full meal. The short menu emphasizes Brussels specialties, and portions are generous. The owner, a wine importer, serves unusually good wine for the price, by the glass or by the bottle. The red walls are hung with large, contemporary paintings, including works by Pierre Alechinsky, and picture windows overlook the pleasant square. A brass plaque marks the table where President Bill Clinton relaxed during a Brussels walkabout. *Grand Sablon 38, tel. 02/512–6476. Reservations not accepted. MC, V.*

$$ AUX MARCHES DE LA CHAPELLE. This very attractive restaurant,
★ opposite the Eglise de la Chapelle near the Grand Sablon, offers brasserie fare of the highest quality, including traditional sauerkraut. One of the Belle Epoque rooms is dominated by a splendid old bar, the other by an enormous open fireplace. *Pl. de la Chapelle 5, tel. 02/512–6891. AE, DC, MC, V. No lunch Sat. Closed Sun. and 3rd wk July–3rd wk Aug.*

$$ LA CLEF DES CHAMPS. Enter this restaurant and discover a corner of Provence on a cobbled street off the Place du Grand Sablon. The blue and yellow decor is set off by watercolors, photographs, and poems of the multitalented chef and owner. His welcoming wife, who sets the stage in the dining room, is a former dentist— the pair met when he went to have a tooth pulled! The cooking is regional French, with dishes including Mediterranean bass in olive oil; lobster gratin; and duck confit. With the charming service and the golden walls, this has to be one of the sunniest places in the city center. *R. de Rollebeek 23, tel. 02/512–1193. AE, DC, MC, V. Closed Sun. and Mon.*

$$ L'IDIOT DU VILLAGE. Don't believe the modest name of this restaurant in the Marolles; it serves excellent food and attracts a loyal clientele. The emphasis is on quality dining in a relaxed atmosphere rather than attracting the "in" crowd, and the decor is kitschy and warmly intimate. Sample dishes include grilled tuna with artichokes and Parmesan, and warm escalope of foie gras with pepper and vanilla. *R. Notre-Seigneur 19, tel. 02/502–5582. AE, DC, MC, V. Closed weekends.*

$$ LE JOUEUR DE FLÛTE. There's only space for 16 diners in this one-man-show restaurant, which offers a single menu each evening. Philippe Van Cappelen named his place after a drawing he picked up at the flea market, and the walls are decorated with musical manuscripts. It's an intimate, candlelit setting near the hulking Palais de Justice, and because of the formula it's only open for one service each evening. For an idea of what the day's menu is, think fillet of bass with mixed vegetables in olive oil, or Mechelen chicken with licorice. *R. de l'Epée 26, tel. 02/513–4311. Reservations essential. MC, V. No lunch. Closed weekends.*

$$ LE LIVING ROOM. A modish restaurant that lives up to much of the hype, this place gets busy late on weekend evenings as night owls arrive to cluster around the bar. A fashionable, uptown crowd haunts the restaurant-cum-club, which is set in an attractive town house with dining on two floors and in the garden. The bar area bustles, while dining rooms at the front are more refined, with plush, modern decor and armchairs in bright-colored velvets.

The menu is international, from Japan (sushi) and France (chicken breast with morels) by way of Thailand (sautéed beef); the wine list is equally diverse. *Ch. de Charleroi 50, tel. 02/534–4434. AE, DC, MC, V. No lunch.*

$$ LES PETITS OIGNONS. This airy 17th-century restaurant, in the heart of the Marolles, has been furnished with plants and bright, modern paintings. It places no demands on your palate, but the ambience is enticing, and you are well looked after. The menu changes every couple of weeks, but staples include fried goose liver with caramelized onions, roast pigeon with carrots and cumin, and leg of lamb with potatoes au gratin. *R. Notre-Seigneur 13, tel. 02/512–4738. AE, DC, MC, V. Closed Sun. and Aug.*

$$ LE SAINT-BONIFACE. Near the church of the same name in Ixelles, this defiantly untrendy restaurant serves wholesome, traditional fare from southern France. The intricacies of duck confit and *andouillette* (sausage made from pig's intestines) will be patiently explained by the friendly wife of the chef. Portions are generous and the setting is classic French bistro, with red-and-white check tablecloths, posters on the walls, and classical music or jazz in the background. *R. St-Boniface 9, tel. 02/511–5366. AE, DC, MC, V. No lunch Sat. Closed Sun.*

$–$$ AMADEUS. It is not so much the food (goat cheese with honey, spare ribs, tagliatelle with salmon) as the decor that makes this converted artist's studio near the Place Stéphanie a must. Ultra-romantic, not to say kitschy, its dining rooms have an abundance of mirrors, candles, and intimate alcoves, creating a trysty, almost conspiratorial baroque feel. *R. Veydt 13, tel. 02/538–3427. AE, DC, MC, V. No lunch. Closed mid-July–mid-Aug.*

$ ADRIENNE. The huge buffet draws crowds year after year at this upstairs restaurant, just around the corner from Avenue Toison d'Or. The look is rustic, with red-and-white check tablecloths; you can eat on the terrace in summer. The location is great for uptown shopping and movies as well as Sunday brunch, and it's also fun for kids. The Atomium branch, which is under different management, is cheaper but of equally good quality. R. Capitaine Crespel 1A, tel. 02/511–9339; Atomium du Heysel, near Atomium, tel. 02/478–3000. AE, DC, MC, V. No dinner Sun.

$ BAZAAR. An taste of exoticism along a side street in the Marolles, this building has an interesting history—it was once a convent—and a tendency to catch fire. That doesn't stop the candles burning in the cavernous dining room, where a beautiful air balloon is suspended over the bar and Moroccan lamps and sofas create intimacy in a bric-a-brac setting. It's young and fashionable, there's a disco on the lower floor at weekends, and monthly concerts of world music are performed here. The eclectic, inexpensive menu includes such choices as chicken tajine (slow-cooked with gravy in a deep, glazed earthenware dish) with olives and lemon and ostrich carpaccio. R. des Capucins 63, tel. 02/511–2600. AE, DC, MC, V. No lunch. Closed Sun. and Mon.

$ DE LA VIGNE À L'ASSIETTE. This homely, no-frills bistro off Avenue
★ Louise opened in early 2000 and offers a food and wine formula that's an exceptionally good value. The modern French cuisine is embellished with such exotic flourishes as star anise sauce with Asian spicing, and grilled salmon topped with crisp angel-hair pastry. Menus, which change with the seasons, include interesting choices like hop shoots topped with a poached egg, and frothy mousseline sauce. The excellent wine list, chosen by co-owner Eddy Dandrimont, a former best sommelier of Belgium, is free of the usual hefty markup. R. de la Longue Haie, tel. 02/647–6803. AE, DC, MC, V. No lunch Sat. Closed Sun. and Mon.

$ GALLERY. This Vietnamese restaurant looks like a minimalist art gallery, with contemporary black chairs and tables, artfully suspended spotlights, and temporary exhibitions of black-and-white photographs. The kitchen holds no surprises, but the food is well prepared and the helpings of dishes such as Vietnamese pancakes, hot-and-sour soup, and beef with chilis and peppers are substantial. *R. du Grand Cerf 7, tel. 02/511–8035. AE, DC, MC, V. No lunch Sun. Closed 1 wk in Aug.*

$ **LA GRANDE PORTE.** A longtime favorite in the Marolles area that makes no concession to fashion or style, this old place has a player piano and offhand but jovial waiters. It serves copious portions of popular Brussels specialties, such as *ballekes à la marollienne* (spicy meatballs) and *carbonnade à la flamande* (beef and onions stewed in beer). The later in the evening it becomes, the livelier the atmosphere and the greater the demand for the restaurant's famous onion soup. *R. Notre-Seigneur 9, tel. 02/512–8998. MC, V. No lunch Sat. Closed Sun.*

CINQUANTENAIRE AND SCHUMAN

$$$ **LA DUCHESSE.** The eatery within the homely Montgomery Hotel offers more than the average hotel restaurant. Chef Yves Defontaine specializes in fish but is extremely creative with vegetables, which he incorporates into inventive, modern French cuisine. Roast fillet of bass with tarragon and fresh-grilled bacon with Guinea pepper is one of the specialities. *Av. de Tervuren 134, tel. 02/741–8511. AE, DC, MC, V. Closed weekends.*

WEST OF CENTER

$$$$ **BRUNEAU.** Although it's outside the city center, this quarter-century-old restaurant is famous with gourmets in Belgium and beyond. They come for top-notch food served in a lavishly decorated town house, or in the garden during summer. The food is complex and ornate, the wine list excellent. Jean-Pierre Bruneau works in the open kitchen and is a master of gastronomic art. His fans swear by his cooking and flex their plastic to prove it. *Av. Broustin 75, tel. 02/427–6978. AE, DC, MC, V. No dinner Tues. Closed Wed., Aug., and 1st wk Feb.*

In This Chapter

Updated by Leslie Adler

shopping

THE BELGIANS STARTED PRODUCING HIGH-QUALITY luxury goods in the Middle Ages, and this is what they are skilled at. This is not a country where you pick up amazing bargains. Value added tax (TVA) further inflates prices, but visitors from outside the European Union can obtain refunds.

DEPARTMENT STORES

The best Belgian department store is **Inno** (R. Neuve 111, tel. 02/211–2111; Av. Louise 12, tel. 02/513–8494; Chaussée de Waterloo 699, tel. 02/345–3890). Others, such as **C&A** and **Marks & Spencer,** are clustered at the Place de la Monnaie end of Rue Neuve, a run-down street that is now undergoing a much-needed face-lift.

SHOPPING DISTRICTS

The stylish, upmarket shopping area for clothing and accessories comprises the upper end of **Avenue Louise** and includes **Avenue de la Toison d'Or,** which branches off at a right angle; **Boulevard de Waterloo,** on the other side of the street; **Galerie Louise,** which links the two avenues; and **Galerie de la Toison d'Or,** another gallery two blocks away. The **City 2** mall on Place Rogier and the pedestrian mall, **Rue Neuve,** are fun and inexpensive shopping areas (but not recommended for women alone after dark). There are galleries scattered across Brussels, but low rents have made **Boulevard Barthélémy** the "in" place for avant-garde art. The **Windows** complex (Bd. Barthélémy 13) houses several galleries. On the **Place du Grand-Sablon** and

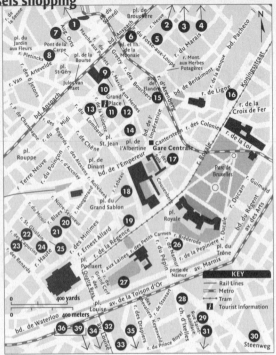

adjoining streets and alleys you'll find antiques dealers and smart art galleries. The **Galeries St-Hubert** is a rather stately shopping arcade lined with upscale shops selling men's and women's clothing, books, and interior design products. In the trendy **Rue Antoine Dansaert** and **Place du Nouveau Marché aux Grains,** near the Bourse, are a number of boutiques carrying fashions by young designers and interior design and art shops. **Place du Chatelaine** and the surrounding streets in Ixelles near Avenue Louise feature a number of upmarket boutiques offering women's and men's clothes, as well as an assortment of other shops, including antiques, housewares, and secondhand clothes.

MARKETS

Bruxellois with an eye for fresh farm produce and low prices do most of their food shopping at the animated open-air markets in almost every borough. Among the best are those in **Boitsfort** in front of the Maison Communal on Sunday morning; on **Place du Châtelain,** Wednesday afternoon; and on **Place Ste-Catherine,** all day, Monday through Saturday. In addition to fruits, vegetables, meat, and fish, most markets include traders with specialized products, such as wide selections of cheese and wild mushrooms. The most exotic market is the Sunday morning **Marché du Midi,** where the large North African community gathers to buy and sell foods, spices, and plants, transforming the area next to the railway station into a vast bazaar.

In the Grand'Place there are a **Flower Market,** daily, except Monday, and a **Bird Market,** Sunday morning. You need to get to the flea market, **Vieux Marché** (Pl. du Jeu de Balle) early. It's open daily 7–2. The **Antiques and Book Market** (Pl. du Grand-Sablon), Saturday 9–6 and Sunday 9–2, is frequented by established dealers.

SPECIALTY STORES

Antiques

For antique bathroom fittings, including deep tubs meant for long soaks and marble washstands go to **Baden Baden** (R. Haute 78–84, tel. 02/548–9690). **La Bobine D'Or** (R. Blaes 135, tel. 02/513–4817) is crammed with antique lace, vintage clothes, jewelry, figurines, and just about anything else that can be squeezed in. **Le Cheverny** (R. Haute 126, tel. 02/511–5495) has a fine selection of art nouveau lamps, as well as some art deco. **Espace 161** (R. Haute 161, tel. 02/502–3164) offers crystal chandeliers and sumptuous furniture. **Le Grenier de la Bourse** (R. Antoine Dansaert 2, tel. 02/512–6879) has an eclectic selection of furniture and objects.

Grenier de la Chapelle (R. Haute 51, tel. 02/513–2955) offers rustic wood furniture. **Lemaire** (R. de la Régence 34, tel. 02/511–0513) has an extensive selection of fine porcelain and earthenware. **Passage 125 Blaes** (R. Blaes 121–125, tel. 02/503–1027) brings together 25 antiques dealers under one roof, with a vast range of goods including chandeliers, bathroom fixtures, art, and furniture in a variety of styles.

Beer

400 bières artisanales (Chaussée de Wavre 175, tel. 02/511–3742), a little off the beaten track, should be visited by anyone with a serious interest in Belgian beer. The owner is friendly and knowledgeable and his selection of ales is well-judged and continually surprising. Don't forget to buy the glass that goes with your *dubbel* or *tripel*.

Books

The **Galerie Bortier** (R. de la Madeleine–R. St-Jean) is a small, attractive arcade devoted entirely to rare and secondhand books. It was designed by the architect responsible for the Galeries St-Hubert. **Librairie des Galeries** (Galerie du Roi 2, tel.

02/511–2412) carries an extensive selection of books in both French and English on art, architecture, and photography. This is the place to find books on topics as specialized as 18th- and 19th-century Belgian pottery.

Libris (Espace Louise, tel. 02/511–6400) is well stocked with current French-language titles. Shops specializing in comic strip albums include those at Chaussée de Wavre Nos. 167, 179, and 198, and the **Tintin Boutique** (R. de la Colline 13, off Grand'Place). **Tropismes** (Galerie des Princes 11, tel. 02/512–8852) carries more than 40,000 titles and will help you find out-of-print books.

English-language bookstores include **La Librairie des Etangs** (Chaussée d'Ixelles 319, Ixelles, tel. 02/646–9786), an international bookseller; **Librairie de Rome** (Av. Louise 50b, tel. 02/511–7937), which has a large selection of foreign newspapers and magazines; **Sterling** (R. du Fosse-aux-Loups 38, tel. 02/223–6223), a friendly store run by a team whose enthusiasm for reading is infectious; and the less personal **Waterstone's** (Bd. Adolphe Max 71–75, tel. 02/219–2708), which carries hardcovers, paperbacks, and periodicals. The *International Herald Tribune* and the *Wall Street Journal* are sold by almost all newsdealers. The Sunday *New York Times* is available at both Librairie de Rome and Waterstone's for a rather princely sum.

Children's Clothes

Bonpoint (Av. Louise 31, tel. 02/534–1640) is the place to go for those who want to spare no expense dressing the little ones like young royalty. For more practical clothes but with a distinctive style, try **Puzzles** (R. Leon Lepage 1, tel. 02/512–1172).

Chocolates

Godiva (Grand'Place 22 and other locations) is the best known, with **Neuhaus** (Galerie de la Reine 25–27 and other locations) a close second. **Leonidas** (Chaussée d'Ixelles 5 and other locations) is the budget alternative, but still high quality thanks to Belgium's strict controls on chocolate. The best handmade pralines, the crème de la crème of Belgian chocolates, are made by **Pierre Marcolini** (Pl. du Grand Sablon 39, tel. 02/514–1206), the boy wonder of the chocolate world; at **Mary** (R. Royale 73, tel. 02/217–4500); and at **Wittamer** (Pl. du Grand Sablon 12, tel. 02/512–3742).

Crystal

The Val St-Lambert mark is the only guarantee of handblown, hand-engraved lead crystal vases and other glass. You can buy it in many stores; the specialist is **Art et Sélection** (R. du Marché-aux-Herbes 83, tel. 02/511–8448).

Food

Maison J. Dandoy (R. au Beurre 31, tel. 02/511–0326) has the best biscuits in Brussels, including the Belgian specialty Speculoos, a spiced cookie available in many shapes and sizes. **Le Palais du Gourmet** (R. du Bailli 106, tel. 02/537–6653) is a gourmet paradise. The temptations include cheeses, condiments, oils and vinegars, foie gras, caviar, and wine. **O&Co.** (R. au Beurre 28, tel. 02/502–7511) is stacked to the ceiling with a wide selection of olive oils made by small producers from throughout the Mediterranean, including France, Italy, Spain, Greece, and Israel. **La Septième Tasse** (R. du Bailli 37, tel. 02/647–1971) sells about 100 different kinds of teas, as well as china teapots and gleaming silver urns. You can enjoy a cup of tea in the shop's cozy café, as well as buy tea to take home.

Hats

Christophe Coppens (R. Léon Lepage 2, tel. 02/512–7797) is a Flemish milliner designing hats on the cutting edge of fashion. If you're planning a trip to Ascot, this is the place to find that one-of-a-kind creation that will make you stand out in a crowd. **Vincenti** (R. du Namur 30, tel. 02/512–7902) sells handmade hats, as well as handbags, scarves and jewelry. Hats may also be custom-ordered.

Lace and Linen

Manufacture Belge de Dentelle (Galerie de la Reine 6–8, tel. 02/511–4477) and **Maison F. Rubbrecht** (Grand'Place 23, tel. 02/512–0218) sell local handmade lace. Lace sold in the souvenir shops is likely to come from East Asia. An introductory visit to the **Musée du Costume et de la Dentelle** (R. de la Violette 6, tel. 02/512–7709) is a good idea if you're planning to shop for lace. For Belgian linen, try **Martine Doly** (Bd. de Waterloo 27, tel. 02/512–4628).

Leather Goods

Delvaux (Galerie de la Reine 31, tel. 02/512–7198; Bd. de Waterloo 27, tel. 02/513–0502) makes outstanding, classic handbags, wallets, belts, and attaché cases. Be prepared to part with a hefty sum, but the Delvaux products last and last.

Men's Clothes

Olivier Strelli (Av. Louise 72, tel. 02/512–5607) caters to the well-dressed set looking for contemporary, minimalist fashion. If you're looking for shirts, head to **Pink** (Bvd. Waterloo 23., tel. 02/502–0508). The selection of shirts and ties is vast, and, yes, they come in many colors in addition to pink. There is also a smaller selection of women's shirts.

Music

La Boite à Musique (R. Ravenstein 17–19, tel. 02/513–0965) is the best place in Brussels for classical music, which is not surprising considering the store's location next to the Palais des Beaux-Arts symphony hall. **FNAC** (City 2, R. Cendres 16, tel. 02/209–2211) offers a full range of music, from rap to rock to jazz, in a large store that also has a good selection of books, in English as well as French. **Virgin Megastore** (Bd. Anspach 30, tel. 02/219–9004) is another good site for the full gamut of musical tastes.

Perfume

Senteurs D'Ailleurs (Av. Louise 100, tel. 02/511–6969) is the Rolls-Royce of perfume shops, with a diverse selection of perfumes, bath products, and candles in scents ranging from floral to thyme and honey from specialized producers.

Tapestries

For tapestries that are evidence of Belgium's long tradition as a high-quality textiles-producing center head for **Textilux Center** (R. du Lombard 41b, tel. 02/513–5015).

Toys

Serneels (Av. Louise 69, tel. 02/538–3066) is a paradise of toys that is as much fun for adults as for children, although the prices tend to be stratospheric. The stuffed animals, many of them virtually life-size and of superb quality, are the stars of the store. But exquisite wooden rocking horses, wooden soldiers, dolls, and model cars, boats, trains, and airplanes add to a setting that's hard to resist.

Women's Clothes

Chine (R. Van Arteveld 2, tel. 02/503–1499), as the name implies, sells clothes from China, mainly simple silks in softly feminine styles. **Kaat Tilley** (Galerie du Roi 4, tel. 02/514–0763) is a Flemish designer selling fanciful designs in a fairy-like setting. Contemporary jewelry of her own design is also for sale. Flemish designer Edouard Vermeulen, who created the elegantly contemporary wedding gown worn by Belgium's Princess Mathilde at her wedding in 1999 to Crown Prince Philippe, is the genius behind **Natan** (Av. Louise 158, tel. 02/647–1001). His clothes feature the minimalist, high-fashion look favored by Flemish designers. Natan also has a second location at Rue du Namur 78, as well as a men's shop on Rue Antoine Dansaert. Designer **Nina Meert** (R. St. Boniface 1, tel. 02/514–2263) comes from a family of painters and opened her house of couture in 1979 in Brussels and Paris. She has dressed the likes of actresses Isabelle Adjani and Meryl Streep and Belgium's Queen Paola.

In This Chapter

Updated by Leslie Adler

outdoor activities and sports

SOCCER, OR FOOTBALL, AS IT'S KNOWN HERE, is by far the most popular sport in Brussels, with horse-racing taking second place. If you are looking for opportunities to exercise, try one of the hotel fitness centers open to the public, a tennis club, or a jog in one of the city's lovely parks.

PARTICIPANT SPORTS
Golf

The top clubs in the area are **Keerbergen Golf Club** (Vlieghavenlaan 50, Keerbergen, tel. 015/234961), **Royal Golf Club de Belgique** (Château de Ravenstein, Tervuren, tel. 02/767–5801), and **Royal Waterloo Golf Club** (Vieux Chemin de Wavre 50, Ohain, tel. 02/633–1850). For more information, call the **Royal Belgian Golf Federation** (tel. 02/672–2389).

Fitness Centers

Several hotels have well-equipped fitness centers open to the public. The most luxurious, and the most expensive is **Champneys,** an English import located in the swank Conrad Hotel. A one-day visit costs BF4,500, offering use of the top-notch facilities as well as classes, lunch, and a half-hour massage (Ave. Louise 71B, tel. 02/542–4666). Other very good and less expensive choices include the **World Class Health Academy** in the Swiss Hôtel (R. du Parnasse 19, tel. 02/551–5990), **John**

Harris Fitness at the Radisson SAS Hotel (R. du Fossé-aux-Loups 47, tel. 02/219-8254), and Sheraton (Pl. Rogier 3, tel. 02/224-3111). Fees average BF1,000 a session. Prices are considerably lower at independent health clubs, such as California Club (R. Lesbroussart 68, tel. 02/640-9344) and European Athletic City (Av. Winston Churchill 25A, tel. 02/345-3077).

Horseback Riding

For outdoor horseback riding, try Le Centre Equestre de la Cambre (Chausée de Waterloo 872, tel. 02/375-3408), Musette (Drève du Caporal 11, tel. 02/374-2591), or Royal Etrier Belge (Champ du Vert Chasseur 19, tel. 02/374-3870).

Jogging

For in-town jogging, use the Parc de Bruxelles (R. de la Loi to the Palace); for more extensive workouts, head for the Bois de la Cambre (Southern end of Av. Louise), a natural park that is a favorite among joggers and families with children. The park merges on the south into the beech woods of the 11,000-acre Forêt de Soignes, extending as far south as Genval with its lake and restaurants.

Swimming

Hotel swimming pools are few and far between. Among covered public pools, the best are Calypso (Av. Wiener 60, tel. 02/663-0090), Longchamp (Sq. de Fré 1, tel. 02/374-9005), and Poseidon (Av. des Vaillants 2, tel. 02/771-6655).

Tennis

Popular clubs include the Royal Léopold (Av. Dupuich 42, tel. 02/344-3666), Royal Racing Club (Av. des Chênes 125, tel. 02/374-4181), and Wimbledon (Waterloosesteenweg 220, Sint-Genesius-Rode, tel. 02/358-3523).

SPECTATOR SPORTS
Horse Racing

Going to the races is second in popularity only to soccer, and there are three major racecourses: **Boitsfort** (Chaussée de la Hulpe 53, tel. 02/675–3015), which has an all-weather flat track; **Groenendael** (Sint-Jansberglaan 4, Hoeilaart, tel. 02/675–3015), for steeplechasing; and **Sterrebeek** (Du Roy de Blicquylaan 43, Sterrebeek, tel. 02/675–5293), for trotting and flat racing between February and June. For more information, contact the **Jockey Club de Belgique** (tel. 02/672–7248).

Soccer

Soccer is Belgium's most popular spectator sport, and the leading club, **Anderlecht,** has many fiercely loyal fans—even despite poor showings in recent seasons and the discovery that club bosses bribed referees during a European competition in the early '80s. Their home field is **Parc Astrid** (Av. Theo Verbeeck 2, tel. 02/522–1539). Major international games are played at the **Stade Roi Baudouin** (Av. du Marathon 135, tel. 02/479–3654). For information and tickets, contact the **Maison du Football** (Av. Houba de Strooper 145, tel. 02/477–1211).

Updated by Katharine Mill

nightlife and the arts

BY 11 PM, MOST BRUXELLOIS have packed up and gone home. But around midnight, bars and cafés fill up again and roads become congested as the night people take over; many places stay open till dawn. By and large, Belgians provide their own entertainment but, while Brussels's nightclubs are not in the same league as London's or Amsterdam's, the scene has been improving for the past few years.

The arts in Brussels are thriving in the wake of the capital's stint as the year 2000 European city of culture. Although the linguistic division drives a wedge through the cultural landscape, the advantage is that funds are injected by both Flemish- and French-language authorities eager to promote their separate contributions. A glance at the "What's On" supplement of weekly English-language newsmagazine *The Bulletin* reveals the breadth of the offerings in all categories of cultural life. Tickets for major events can be purchased by calling **Fnac Ticket Line** (tel. 0900/00600).

NIGHTLIFE
Bars and Lounges

Although the Belgian brewing industry is declining, Belgians still consume great quantities of beer, some of it with a 10% alcohol content. You'll find a variety of brews, as well as other types of alcoholic beverages, in the city's many bars and cafés. The sidewalk outside **Au Soleil** (86 R. du Marché-au-Charbon) teems with the hip and would-be hip, enjoying relaxed trip-hop sounds and very competitive prices. Fashionable Flemings, meanwhile, flock to the **Beurs Café** (R. Auguste Orts 20–26), a huge, minimalist hall with a friendly atmosphere next door to the innovative Beursschouwburg cultural center. The **Archiduc** (R. Dansaert 6) attracts a thirtyish fashion crowd in its stylish art deco abode, though it gets smoky up on the balcony.

Chez Moeder Lambic (R. de Savoie 68, St-Gilles) claims to stock 600 Belgian beers and a few hundred more foreign ones. **De Ultieme Hallucinatie** (R. Royale 316) is an art nouveau masterpiece, with a pricey restaurant as well as a roomy tavern. **Fleur en Papier Doré** (R. des Alexiens 53) was the hangout for Surrealist René Magritte and his artist friends, and their spirit lingers on. At the tiny **Java** (R. de la Grande Ile 22), the bar is shaped like a huge anaconda. On the Grand'Place, **'t Kelderke** (Grand'Place 15) is a bustling, friendly option. In the trendy Place Saint-Géry district, **Zebra** (Pl. St-Géry 35) attracts a comfortably fashionable crowd, while **Mappa Mundo** (R. du Pont de la Carpe 2–6) on the opposite corner packs two floors with an international mix of revelers and poseurs. On warm nights, it's difficult to find a table.

Brussels's sizable French-speaking black population, hailing mostly from the Republic of Congo (the former Zaire), congregates in the area of Ixelles known as Matonge. **Chaussée de Wavre** is the principal street for African shops, bars, and restaurants. The nearby **Ultime Atome** (R. St-Boniface 14, tel. 02/511–1367) is a fashionable neighborhood bar-restaurant that's busy day and night (and serves food until 1 AM). **L'Amour Fou** (Ch. d'Ixelles 185, tel. 02/514–2709) has a selection of newspapers for the lone visitor and is popular with the student intellectual crowd.

There are a number of favored Anglo-expat hangouts in Brussels. **Conway's** (Av. de la Toison d'Or tel. 02/511–2668) is a singles bar where the staff's ice-breaking activities are the stuff of local legend. **Rick's Café Américain** (Av. Louise 344, tel. 02/648–1451) is flashy and does Sunday brunch.

Like most western European cities, Brussels has a sizable number of "Irish" bars: **The James Joyce** (R. Archimède 34, tel. 02/230–9894), **Kitty O'Shea's** (Bd. de Charlemagne 42, tel. 02/230–7875), the heaving **Wild Geese** (Av. Livingstone 2-4, tel. 02/230–1990), and **O'Reilly's** (Pl. de la Bourse, tel. 02/552–0481). Among the most popular hotel bars are those in the **Hilton,** the **Amigo,** and the **Métropole** (☞ Eating Out and Where to Stay).

Cabarets

Transvestite shows spark **Chez Flo** (R. au Beurre 25, tel. 02/512–9496). **La Voix Secrète** (R. du Lombard 1, tel. 02/511–5679) does food in a gothic atmosphere with costumed waiters and a musical floor show from Wednesday to Sunday. At **Show Point** (Pl. Stephanie 14, tel. 02/511–5364) the draw is striptease.

Dance Clubs

The dance scene is in perpetual mutation: as fast as a promising new outfit sets up, another falls foul of regulations and shuts down. Look out for posters announcing hot nights—sometimes in obscure venues like the bowels of the Gare Centrale or even the Atomium. Action starts at midnight in most clubs.

Salsa addicts can indulge their habit at **Cartagena** (R. du Marché-au-Charbon 70, tel. 02/502–5908) or the **Montecristo Café** (R. Henri Maus 25, tel. 02/511–8789). Electronica fans prefer **Fuse** (R. Blaes 208, tel. 511–9789), a bunker-style techno haven with monthly gay nights. **Mirano Continental** (Chaussée de Louvain 38, tel. 02/227–3970) remains the glitzy hangout of choice for the self-styled beautiful people, while an affluent set retreat to the **Jeux d'Hiver** (Chemin du Croquet 1, tel. 02/649–0864), hidden among trees in the Bois de la Cambre. **Tour & Taxi** (R. Picard 6) puts on thumping house and one-off events in the impressive hulk of a former customs depot whose future is decidedly uncertain.

Gay Bars

Brussels is not nearly as advanced as Amsterdam when it comes to gay culture, but several clubs hold regular gay and lesbian nights. La Démence is the monthly gay night at **Fuse** (☞ Dance Clubs, *above*). **Belgica** (R. du Marché-au-Charbon 32) is a trendy meeting point at the heart of what passes for the gay quarter; **Strong** (R. Ste-Christophe 1) is a bar and club from Thursday to Saturday. **Tels Quels** (R. du Marché-aux-Charbon 81, tel. 02/512–4587) is a social service that publishes a monthly magazine as well as a bar and can offer up-to-date information about the capital's gay scene. For lesbians, the **Café qu'on sert** (Av. Albert 59, tel. 02/343–0233) or **Le Capricorne** (R. d'Anderlecht 6, tel. 02/512–1503) are the best bets.

Jazz

After World War II, Belgium was at the forefront of Europe's modern jazz movement: of the great postwar players, harmonica maestro Toots Thielemans and vibes player Sadi are still very much alive and perform in Brussels. Other top Belgian jazz draws include guitarist Philip Catherine and the experimental ethno-jazz trio Aka Moon. Among the best jazz venues are **L'Archiduc** (R. Antoine Dansaert 6, tel. 02/512–0652), the **New York Café Jazz Club** (Chaussée de Charleroi 5, tel. 02/534–8509), **Sounds** (R. de la Tulipe 28, tel. 02/512–9250), and **Travers** (R. Traversière 11, tel. 02/218–4086).

Mainstream rock acts and big-league French chansonniers stop off at **Forest-National** (Av. du Globe 36, tel. 02/340–2211). **Ancienne Belgique** (Bd. Anspach 110, tel. 02/548–2424) hosts a wide range of rock, pop, alternative, and world music, as does **Le Botanique** (R. Royale 236, tel. 02/218–3732), which has a superb 10-day festival, *Les Nuits Botanique*, in September. Though officially the Galician cultural centre, **La Tentation** (R. de Laeken 28, tel. 02/223–2275) hosts a broad selection of world music performers in a superb venue, while **Fool Moon Theatre** (Quai de Mariemont

26, tel. 02/410–1003) headlines artists playing drum'n'bass, trip-hop and other funky sounds, continuing into the night as a dance club. For up-and-coming British and European alternative bands, try **VK** (R. de l'Ecole 76, tel. 02/414–2907).

THE ARTS
Film

First-run English-language and French movies predominate: the Belgian film industry is small but of high quality. At the 1999 Cannes Film Festival, director brothers Luc and Jean-Pierre Dardenne won the Palme d'Or for "Rosetta," a deadbeat tale set in Líge; directors Jaco Van Dormael, Alain Berliner, Gérard Corbiau, and Stijn Coninx have also achieved international acclaim.

In summer, the excellent cinema **Arenberg/Galeries** (Galeries St-Hubert, tel. 0900/29550) hosts the Ecran Total (Total Cinema) festival, which screens classic Hollywood and French movies alongside new talent from around the world. The most convenient movie theater complexes are **UGC/Acropole** (Av. de la Toison d'Or, tel. 0900/29930) and **UGC/De Brouckère** (Pl. de Brouckère, tel. 0900/29930). Art-house films show at the **Vendôme** (Chaussée de Wavre 18, tel. 0900/29909), which also puts on regular themed festivals (e.g., Latin American or Jewish cinema). The small **Actor's Studio** (Petite rue des Bouchers 16, tel. 0900/27854) shows second-run and art-house films.

The avant-garde **Nova** (R. d'Arenberg 3, tel. 02/511–2774) shows a quirky, uncommercial selection of animation, shorts, and sound installations despite its shoestring budget and uncertain tenancy. The biggest, with 26 theaters, is the futuristic **Kinepolis** (Av. du Centenaire 1, Heysel, tel. 02/474–2604). The **Musée du Cinéma** (R. Baron Horta 9, tel. 02/507–8370) shows classic and silent movies, the latter accompanied live by an improvising pianist. It is one of the only places in the world that shows silent movies daily. Buying a ticket to see a film also gains entry to the small but fascinating museum (BF60 24 hours in advance; BF90 at door). In March, the International Festival of Fantasy Film takes over **Auditorium Passage 44** (Bld. du Jardin Botanique 44, tel. 02/201–1495) and other venues for a packed program of thrillers and chillers, culminating in a Vampires Ball.

Classical Music

The principal venue for classical music concerts is the Horta-designed **Palais des Beaux-Arts** (R. Ravenstein 23, tel. 02/507–8200). The complex, which also houses the Film Museum, an art gallery, and a theater, was the first multipurpose arts complex in Europe when it opened in 1928. Its Henry Le Boeuf concert hall has been restored to world-class acoustic standards since recent renovations corrected some earlier misguided alterations. Chamber music concerts and recitals are held in the more intimate **Royal Conservatory** (R. de la Régence 30, tel. 02/507–8200). Many concerts are held in churches, especially the **Chapelle Protestante** (Pl. du Musée) and the **Eglise des Minimes** (R. des Minimes 62).

Belgium is particularly renowned in the fields of early and Baroque music—look out for conductors René Jacobs and Philippe Herreweghe and the Sablon Baroque Spring festival in April/May. Also in spring, the grueling **Queen Elisabeth Music Competition** (the penultimate round is at the Royal Conservatory, the final week at the Palais des Beaux-Arts), a prestigious competition for young pianists, violinists, and singers, takes place in Brussels. The monthlong **Ars Musica** (tel. 02/512–1717) festival of contemporary music in March and April attracts new music ensembles from around the world. The best new music group in Belgium is the Ictus Ensemble, which pops up all over the place, especially in collaboration with dance troupes.

Opera and Dance

The national opera house is the excellent **La Monnaie/De Munt** (Pl. de la Monnaie, tel. 02/218–1211). This is where the 1830 revolution started: inflamed by the aria starting "Amour sacré de la patrie" (Sacred love of your country) in Auber's *La Muette de Portici*, members of the audience rushed outside and started rioting. The brief and largely bloodless revolution against the Dutch established the Belgian nation. Visiting opera and dance companies often perform at **Cirque Royal** (R. de l'Enseignement 81, tel. 02/218–2015).

Dance is among the liveliest arts in Belgium. Its seminal figure, Anne Teresa De Keersmaeker, is choreographer-in-residence at the opera house, but her Rosas company also has its own performance space within her **PARTS school** (Av. Van Volxem 164, tel. 02/344–5598). Alternatively, it performs at the **Lunatheater** (Pl. Sainctelette 20, tel. 02/201–5959), as do the Royal Flanders Ballet and many other Belgian and international dance troupes. Innovative provincial company Charleroi/Danses opened **La Raffinerie** (R. de Manchester, tel. 02/410–3341), a new Brussels base, in a splendid old sugar refinery in Molenbeek. The delightful **Chapelle des Brigittines** (R. des Visitandines 1, tel. 02/506–4300) welcomes cutting-edge productions.

Theater

Nearly all the city's 30-odd theaters stage French-language plays; only a few present plays in Dutch. Talented amateur groups also put on occasional English-language performances, and top British companies, including the Royal Shakespeare Company, are becoming regular visitors.

Avant-garde performances are often the most rewarding and show at the **Lunatheater** (☞ Opera and Dance, *above*), **Théâtre Les Tanneurs** (R. des Tanneurs 75, tel. 02/512–1784), and **Théâtre de Poche** (Chemin du Gymnase 1a, tel. 02/649–1727).

Not a Night Owl?

You can learn a lot about a place if you take its pulse after dark. So even if you're the original early-to-bed type, there's every reason to vary your routine when you're away from home.

EXPERIENCE THE FAMILIAR IN A NEW PLACE Whether your thing is going to the movies or going to concerts, it's always different away from home. In clubs, new faces and new sounds add up to a different scene. Or you may catch movies you'd never see at home.

TRY SOMETHING NEW Do something you've never done before. It's another way to dip into the local scene. A simple suggestion: Go out later than usual—go dancing late and finish up with breakfast at dawn.

DO SOMETHING OFFBEAT Look into lectures and readings as well as author appearances in book stores. You may even meet your favorite novelist.

EXPLORE A DAYTIME NEIGHBORHOOD AT NIGHT Take a nighttime walk through an explorable area you've already seen by day. You'll get a whole different view of it.

ASK AROUND If you strike up a conversation with like-minded people during the course of your day, ask them about their favorite spots. Your hotel concierge is another resource.

DON'T WING IT As soon as you've nailed down your travel dates, look into local publications or surf the Net to see what's on the calendar while you're in town. Look for hot regional acts, dance and theater, big-name performing artists, expositions, and sporting events. Then call or click to order tickets.

CHECK OUT THE NEIGHBORHOOD Whenever you don't know the neighborhood you'll be visiting, review safety issues with people in your hotel. What's the transportation situation? Can you walk there, or do you need a cab? Is there anything else you need to know?

CASH OR CREDIT? Know before you go. It's always fun to be surprised—but not when you can't cover your check.

Check what's on at **Rideau de Bruxelles** (Palais des Beaux-Arts, R. Ravenstein 23, tel. 02/507–8200), **Théâtre Le Public** (R. Braemt 64–70, tel. 0800/94444), **Théâtre National** (Pl. Rogier, tel. 02/203–5303), **Théâtre des Martyrs** (Pl. des Martyrs 22, tel. 02/223–3208), and **Théâtre Varia** (R. du Sceptre 78, tel. 02/640–8258).

The annual Kunsten **FESTIVALdesArts** contemporary arts festival (produced by both Flemish and French-language communities) takes place in May in numerous venues and puts on a cutting-edge selection of theater, music, dance, multimedia, and visual arts from Belgium and abroad.

In This Chapter

Updated by Katharine Mill

where to stay

AS THE CAPITAL OF EUROPE, Brussels attracts a large number of high-powered visitors—one in two travelers are here on business—hence, a disproportionate number of very attractive luxury hotels have been built to accommodate them. Their prices are higher than what most tourists would like to pay, but on weekends and during July and August, when there aren't many business travelers, prices can drop to below BF5,000 for a double room. As a rule though, always negotiate a price: the listed rate is rarely applied in practice in the larger hotels.

Happily, new hotels catering to cost-conscious travelers, priced at less than BF3,000 for a double, have also been constructed over the last few years. They may be less ostentatious, but they're squeaky-clean and offer as much attention to your comfort as the palatial five-star hotels. The service in moderately priced establishments is sometimes criticized, but if you come with an open mind and a smile, you probably won't be greatly disappointed.

CATEGORY	COST*
$$$$	over BF9,000/€225
$$$	BF6,500–BF9,000/€160–€225
$$	BF3,500–BF6,500/€85–€160
$	under BF3,500/€85

*for two persons sharing double room, including service and tax

LOWER TOWN

$$$$ **AMIGO.** Just a block from the Grand'Place and decorated in
★ Spanish Renaissance style with touches of Louis XV, the Amigo
looks more turn-of-the-20th-century than 1950s, when it was
built. Rooms vary in furnishings, size, and price; those on higher
floors, with views over the surrounding rooftops, are more
expensive. The Presidential Suite has a large terrace overlooking
the Grand'Place. Taken over in 2000 by Sir Rocco Forte, the hotel
is known for its understated luxury and is popular with celebrities.
The service is excellent. *R. d'Amigo 1–3, B1000, tel. 02/547–4747,
fax 02/502–2805. 178 rooms, 7 suites. Restaurant, bar, meeting rooms,
parking (fee). AE, DC, MC, V. www.hotelamigo.com*

$$$$ **BEDFORD.** This hotel has been rebuilt and modified since the
current owners took over in 1955. It stands on the site of a hotel
that, according to legend, was frequented by Luftwaffe and RAF
pilots in Brussels for romantic trysts during and after World War
II. A family-run place, it has a grand, wide lobby with marble
pillars, thick pink carpeting in corridors, and rooms with pink decor
and carpets and cherry-wood furniture. All have telephone, TV,
and minibar. Bathrooms are small but sparkling in cream marble;
10 rooms have only showers. *R. du Midi 135, B1000, tel. 02/512–7840,
fax 02/514–1759. 321 rooms. Restaurant, bar, meeting rooms, parking
(fee). AE, DC, MC, V. www.hotelbedford.com*

$$$$ **LE PLAZA.** Inspired by the George V in Paris, the Plaza opened in
★ 1930 and has maintained a grandiose reputation. Pillaged by the
Germans at the end of World War II, it closed in 1976, reopening
20 years later after exceptional refurbishment. The hotel has
fittings of outstanding quality, from the new corridor carpet made
using the pattern of the original, to rooms decorated with the
greatest attention to taste and detail: elegant wide sinks in the
bathrooms, framed illustrations, cream standard lamps. All have
private fax lines, modem connection, and bathrobes. Deluxe

rooms and suites have free access to the neighboring Fitness Factory. The bar-restaurant is in a grand, high-ceilinged room with a domed roof; the breakfast room is in a palatial room done in apricot and red. But the real treasure is the hotel's historic theater, a former cinema that is now used for conferences, banquets, and presentations. *Bd. Adolphe Max 118-126, B1000, tel. 02/227–6736, fax 02/223–7929. 176 rooms, 17 suites. Bar, restaurant, in-room data ports, in-room safes, exercise room, meeting rooms, parking (fee). AE, DC, MC, V. www.leplaza-brussels.be*

$$$$ MÉTROPOLE. Stepping into this classic hotel, you would think you were boarding the *Orient Express*. The hotel, built in 1895, has been restored to the palace it was during the Belle Epoque. The lobby sets the tone, with its enormously high coffered ceiling, chandeliers, marble, Oriental rugs, and old-fashioned wood-paneled elevator. The theme is carried through in the bar, with potted palms, deep leather sofas, and Corinthian columns; in the café, which opens onto the sidewalk of Place de Brouckère; and in the Alban Chambon restaurant (named for the architect). The rooms are understated modern in varying shades of pastel (some with trompe l'oeil murals), with furniture upholstered in the same material as the bedspreads. *Pl. de Brouckère 31, B1000, tel. 02/217–2300, fax 02/218–0220. 400 rooms, 10 suites. Restaurant, bar, café, health club, convention center, free parking. AE, DC, MC, V.*

$$$$ RADISSON SAS HOTEL. Near the northern end of the Galeries St-★ Hubert, this hotel is decorated in a variety of styles—Asian (wicker furniture and Asian art), Italian (art deco fixtures and furnishings), and Scandinavian (light-wood furniture and parquet flooring). The greenery-filled atrium incorporates a 10-ft-high section of the 12th-century city wall. The Sea Grill is a first-rate seafood restaurant, and Danish open-face sandwiches are served in the atrium's café. A copious buffet breakfast is included. There's no extra charge for children under 15. *R. du Fossé-aux-Loups 47, B1000, tel. 02/219–2828, fax 02/219–6262. 261 rooms, 20 suites. 2 restaurants, bar, sauna,*

central brussels lodging

KEY
— Rail Lines
▭ Metro
┄ Tram
ℹ Tourist Information

pl. du Jardin aux Fleurs
r. Pletinckx
r. 't Kint
r. de la Senne
r. Camusel
r. Van Artevelde
r. des Riches Claires
r. des 6 Jetons
Jules van Praet
pl. St-Géry
r. Antoine Dansaert
bd. Anspach
porte d'Anderlecht
r. d'Anderlecht
r. de Cureghem
r. du Vautour
r. de la Verdure
r. P. de Champagne
pl. Anneessens
r. des
r. du Midi
r. de la Violette
r. de l'Étuve Lombard
r. du Chêne
St.
ch. de Mons
r. Plantin
r. Otlet
r. Brogniez
r. des Foulons
bd. R. Poincaré
bd. du Midi
bd. Maurice Lemonnier
pl. Rouppe
r. du Midi
Bogards
r. des Alexiens
pl. de Dinant
r. des Aleniens
r. d'Accoly
pl. de la Constitution
av. de Stalingrad
r. Terre Neuve
r. du Poinçon
r. Notre-Seigneur
r. Blaes
r. Haute
r. Rollebe
sq. de l'Aviation
rue de l'Autonomie
pl. Bara
bd. Jamar
av. de la Porte de Hal
bd. de l'Europe
Gare du Midi
av. Fonsny
r. de l'Argonne
r. de Russie
rue de Hollande
rue d'Angleterre
r. du Lavoir
r. des Tanneurs
St. Ghislain
r. du Miroir
r. de l'Economie
r. des Capucins
r. des Renards
r. Pieremans
r. Haute
r. des Minime
r. Ernes

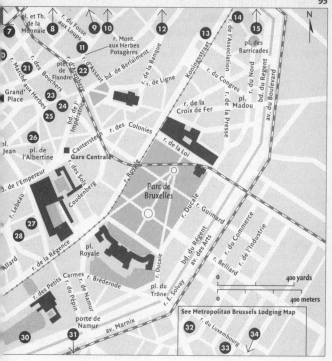

Radisson SAS Hotel, **11**	Sofitel Toison d'Or, **29**
Royal Crown Grand Mercure, **15**	Stanhope, **32**
	Sun, **31**
Royal Windsor Hotel, **26**	Swissôtel, **34**
	Vendôme, **9**
Scandic Grand'Place, **22**	Welcome Hotel, **7**

health club, business services, convention center, parking (fee). AE, DC, MC, V. www.radisson.com/brusselsbe

$$$$ ROYAL WINDSOR HOTEL. Near the Grand'Place and favored by visiting dignitaries, this hotel has survived for more than a quarter century. All rooms have blond-wood paneling, and although the bathrooms are small they're done in Portuguese marble and are among the most beautiful in Brussels. The lobby is businesslike, with leafy plants, comfortable sofas and chairs placed around marble-top tables, and music wafting in from the adjacent piano bar. The elegant dining room, Les Quatre Saisons, serves light, imaginative, and expensive French cuisine; the Windsor Arms is an English-style pub. R. Duquesnoy 5, B1000, tel. 02/505–5555, fax 02/505–5500. 223 rooms, 43 suites. Restaurant, bar, sauna, health club, dance club, convention center, parking (fee). AE, DC, MC, V. www.warwickhotels.com

$$–$$$ NOVOTEL OFF GRAND'PLACE. A stone's throw from the Grand'Place, this 1989 hotel was built with an old-style, gabled facade. Some French lodging chains mass-produce hotels that are functional but motel-like inside, and this is no exception. The rooms have white walls, russet carpets, and a sofa bed (extra guests BF500 per night). Twenty executive rooms are also available. There's no extra charge for up to two children under 16. R. du Marché-aux-Herbes 120, B1000, tel. 02/514–3333, fax 02/511–7723. 136 rooms. Restaurant, bar, meeting rooms, parking (fee). AE, DC, MC, V.

$$ ARLEQUIN. This pleasant, unpretentious hotel in the heart of the Ilot Sacré tourist area has undergone a renovation of all its rooms and common areas. Well-lighted rooms have large TVs, cream-color bamboo fittings, and Impressionist prints; some bathrooms have only showers. Buffet breakfasts are served in the panoramic Septième Ciel (Seventh Heaven) restaurant, which has views over the rooftops to the spires of the Town Hall and Cathedral. The basement bar is '70s chic, all curved walls, red velvet benches, and club chairs, with a wood-and-brushed-steel bar. A jazz band plays several nights a week. The Actors Studio cinema in the same arcade shows second-run and art-house movies. *R. de la Fourche, 17–19, B1000, tel. 02/514–1614, fax 02/514–2202. 92 rooms. Bar, breakfast room, in-room data ports (some), in-room VCRs, meeting rooms. AE, DC, MC, V.*

$$ ATLAS. This hotel offers comfort and unpretentious surroundings in a building dating from the 18th century. Rooms have cream walls, grey carpets, and blue-and-white furniture. Suites, on two floors, each have a kitchenette in the lounge area. Buffet breakfasts are served in the blue-and-white basement with abstract art and the exposed brick of an ancient city wall. There's no bar, but all rooms have minibars and drinks are served on weekday evenings. Cheaper weekend rates are offered for Internet bookings, subject to availability. *R. du Vieux Marché aux Grains 30, B1000, tel. 02/502–6006, fax 02/502–6935. 83 rooms, 5 suites. Breakfast room, minibars, meeting room, parking (fee). AE, DC, MC, V. www.atlas-hotel.be*

$$ CITADINES SAINTE-CATHERINE. This residential apartment hotel also accepts guests staying for a single night. The whitewashed surfaces are offset by bright red details. Rooms, which are more studios and apartments than classic hotel rooms, have pull-out twin beds; junior suites sleep four. All have fully equipped kitchenettes. Rooms on the courtyard are the quietest. *Quai au Bois-à-Brûler 51, B1000, tel. 02/221–1411, fax 02/221–1599. 169 rooms. Kitchenettes, meeting rooms, parking (fee). AE, DC, MC, V. www.citadines.com*

$$ COMFORT ART HOTEL SIRU. All rooms and corridors in this chain hotel contain original work by a Belgian artist. Numbering 130, the works vary from enormous wall murals to fake granite blocks hanging from the ceiling above the bed. The effect runs from refined to truly kitsch but makes for a fun stay. In contrast to the unique embellishments, furnishings are functional and bathrooms are plainly white-tiled. Rooms at the back are quieter but only have a view on higher floors. The art deco building is on a square at the end of pedestrian shopping mecca Rue Neuve. Breakfast is served in the adjoining but independent brasserie. Pl. Rogier 1, B1210, tel. 02/203–3580, fax 02/203–3303. 101 rooms. Minibars, 2 no-smoking floors, parking (fee). AE, DC, MC, V.

$$ LE DIXSEPTIÈME. ★ This hotel between the Grand'Place and Gare Centrale (Central Station) occupies the stylishly restored 17th-century residence of the Spanish ambassador. Rooms surround a pleasant interior courtyard, and suites are up a splendid Louis XVI staircase. Named after Belgian artists, rooms have whitewashed walls, plain floorboards, exposed beams, suede sofas, colorful draperies, desks, blow-dryers, and second telephones. Suites have decorative fireplaces. R. de la Madeleine 25, B1000, tel. 02/502–5744, fax 02/502–6424. 24 rooms. Bar, kitchenettes, in-room data ports, in-room safes, meeting room. AE, DC, MC, V. www.ledixseptieme.be

$$ VENDÔME. Opposite Waterstone's bookshop and a stone's throw from the capital's main pedestrian shopping street is this unpretentious hotel. It's owned by the same Belgian chain as the Madeleine, and the bright rooms have similar fittings: table lamps, green bamboo furniture, and white-tiled bathrooms. All have a bathroom, telephone, minibar, small TV, and desk. Those in the "business category" also have air-conditioning and in-room data ports, and are slightly larger. Rooms at the back are quieter. A hot and cold buffet breakfast is taken in the glass-roofed Veranda room. The restaurant serves brasserie fare. Sightseeing tours can be booked at reception. Bd. Adolphe Max 98, B1000, tel. 02/227–0300, fax 02/218–0683. 99 rooms, 7 suites. Restaurant, bar, in-room data ports, minibars, meeting rooms, parking (fee). AE, DC, MC, V. www.hotel-vendome.be

$–$$ MADELEINE. A brick facade is the public exterior of this modest but friendly hotel that is part of the small, Belgian, Belhotel chain. Between the Central Station and the Grand'Place, it sits just off the bustling Place Agora with its crafts market, buskers, and pavement cafés. Rooms have pale yellow walls, green carpets, and green bamboo furniture. Those at the back have no view but are quieter. The white-tiled bathrooms are compact; small baths have shower attachments. The green and white breakfast room looks out to the square. *R. de la Montagne 20-22, B1000, tel. 02/513–2973, fax 02/502–1350. 52 rooms. Breakfast room. AE, DC, MC, V.*

$ GEORGE V. Located in a central, residential area, this ivy-bedecked hotel is a quiet, English-style hotel in a large house dating from 1859. Rooms, which accommodate up to four people, are simple but spacious, bright, and clean. All have telephones, TVs, and private bathrooms—though some have a deep shower tub rather than a bath. The homey breakfast room has checkered tablecloths, wicker chairs, and a dark pink carpet. *R. t' Kint 23, B1000, tel. 02/513–5093, fax 02/513–4493. 16 rooms. Bar, breakfast room, parking (fee). AE, MC, V. users.skynet.be/george5*

$ GRANDE CLOCHE. This well-appointed family hotel occupies a south-facing corner on a square between the Gare du Midi and the Grand'Place. The green and white facade and yellow entrance hall are fresh and welcoming. Some rooms have a shower but no toilet, others have a full bathroom with separate toilet, and there's a shared hair dryer in the corridor for those who don't have one in their room. Carpets and bedspreads are green, and the walls are beige above a carpeted lower half. The back rooms are particularly peaceful. The ground-floor breakfast room is decorated in springlike green and yellow and has lead-light windows. *Pl. Rouppe 10, B1000, tel. 02/512–6140, fax 02/512–6591. 37 rooms. Breakfast room, parking (fee). AE, MC, V. hotelgrandecloche.com*

$ MATIGNON. Only the facade was preserved in the conversion of this Belle Epoque building to a hotel in 1993. The lobby is no more than a corridor, making room for the large café-brasserie that is part of the family-owned operation. Rooms are small but have generous beds, hair dryers, and large-screen TVs, a welcome change from the dinky TVs you find in most other European budget hotels. Recently added rooms are decorated in salmon and with floral prints. Windows are double-glazed, vital in this busy spot across the street from the Bourse and two blocks from the Grand'Place. *R. de la Bourse 10, B1000, tel. 02/511–0888, fax 02/513–6927. 37 rooms. Restaurant, bar. AE, DC, MC, V.*

$ NOGA. ★ This little hotel has a popular address in the charming Béguinage quarter near the Ste-Catherine fish market. Opened in 1958, the exceptionally well-maintained Noga has earthenware tubs of greenery along the facade, while ornaments and pictures inside evoke the Jazz Age, from table lamps to the black-and-white photographs of the period. Easy chairs in warm yellows and reds adorn the cluttered but cozy lobby area. There are rooms on four floors for two, three, or four people—larger rooms have sofas—and all have bathrooms with shower only. Natural light floods the breakfast room–bar. *R. du Béguinage 38, B1000, tel. 02/218–6763, fax 02/218–1603. 19 rooms. Bar, breakfast room, recreation room, parking (fee). AE, DC, MC, V. www.nogahotel.com*

$ PACIFIC SLEEPING. A noteworthy budget option on the most fashionable street in town, the quirky Pacific is run by the elderly Monsieur Powells. The 1892 building is a treasure trove of early 20th-century style—the breakfast-room decor hasn't changed since his forebears opened the place in 1901. Belgium's colonial past is evoked by the zebra skin that hangs behind the counter of the wood-paneled room with chandeliers and a wallpapered ceiling; an eclectic assortment of artwork clutters the walls here and throughout the hotel. Rooms have old furniture and no bathrooms, but all boast antique china sinks, some double. The shared toilet facilities are spotless; use of the shower costs extra, and there's a midnight curfew. A substantial Belgian breakfast of omelets and cheese is included in the room price. A courteous and informative welcome is guaranteed. *R. Dansaert 57, B1000, tel. 02/511–8459. 15 rooms. Breakfast room. No credit cards.*

$ LA VIEILLE LANTERNE. More bed-and-breakfast than hotel, this tiny, old place of six rooms is run by the family that owns the gift shops on the ground floor. All rooms look out onto the street and the crowds that cluster round the famous Manneken Pis fountain opposite; each has a bathroom with shower only. Fresh and clean with solid-wood, cottagey furniture and lead-light windows in tints of pink, green, and yellow, they are bright and have linoleum floors. Breakfast is served in the rooms. *R. des Grands Carmes 29, B1000, tel. 02/512–7494, fax 02/512–1397. 6 rooms. Shop. AE, DC, MC, V.*

$ **WELCOME HOTEL.** Among the charms of the smallest hotel in Brussels are the young owners, Michel and Sophie Smeesters. The six rooms, divided into economy, business, and first class and with king- or queen-size beds, are as comfortable as those in far more expensive establishments. This little hotel, located in the center of Brussels near the fish market, is much in demand, so book early. There's a charming breakfast room and around the corner on the fish market, Michel doubles as chef of the excellent seafood restaurant La Truite d'Argent ($$$), where hotel guests get a special rate. *R. du Peuplier 5, B1000, tel. 02/219–9546, fax 02/217–1887. 6 rooms. 2 restaurants, meeting room, free parking. AE, DC, MC, V. www.hotelwelcome.com*

UPPER TOWN

$$$$ **ASTORIA.** Built a year before the Brussels World Fair in 1910, the Astoria is a grand hotel in Belle Epoque style. Its checkered history has seen glittering banquets and illustrious guests (Winston Churchill, Salvador Dali, and the wife of the Aga Khan, whose bath was filled with ass's milk), as well as occupation by German forces in both World Wars. Now in the hands of the Sofitel chain, its traditions are still respected, with modernizing touches such as air-conditioning achieved without visible effect. The vast, imposing entrance hall and wide, elegant staircase are noteworthy, as is the Pullman Bar, modeled on the Orient Express, and the Waldorf Room, where classical concerts are held each Sunday at lunchtime. The original bedrooms are much more spacious than those in modern hotels and have high ceilings, period furniture, and

metropolitan brussels lodging

chandeliers. Breakfast is in the Palais Royal restaurant. *R. Royale 103, B1000, tel. 02/227–0505, fax 02/217–1150. 125 rooms, 14 suites. Restaurant, bar, in-room data ports, exercise room, concert hall, meeting rooms, parking (fee). AE, DC, MC, V. www.sofitel.com*

$$$$ CONRAD. The classic facade of an 1865 mansion was combined with a sleek, deluxe American interior in this hotel on the elegant Avenue Louise. Rooms come in many different shapes, but all are spacious and have three telephones, a desk, bathrobes, and in-room checkout. The intimate, gourmet Maison de Maître restaurant is well respected, while Café Wiltcher's offers all-day brasserie dining. The large piano bar is pleasantly chummy. A branch of the exclusive English health club Champneys located in the basement offers all manner of beauty treatments as well as the usual gym facilities. *Av. Louise 71, B1050, tel. 02/542–4242, fax 02/542–4300. 269 rooms, 15 suites. 2 restaurants, 2 bars, health club, shops, convention center, parking (fee). AE, DC, MC, V. www.brussels.conradinternational.com*

$$$$ HILTON. One of the first high-rises in Brussels back in the 1960s, this one outclasses most other Hiltons in Europe and is continuously being refurbished floor by floor. The four stories of executive rooms have a separate check-in area; there are nine floors of business rooms. The location is great for upscale shopping, and the building has a fine panoramic view over the capital. The first-floor restaurant, the Maison du Boeuf, is one of the best in town; the ground-floor Café d'Egmont stays open around the clock. *Bd. de Waterloo 38, B1000, tel. 02/504–1111, fax 02/504–2111. 431 rooms, 39 suites. 2 restaurants, bar, sauna, exercise room, shops, convention center, parking (fee). AE, DC, MC, V. www.hilton.com*

$$$$ SOFITEL TOISON D'OR. The six-floor Sofitel has a great location opposite the Hilton. There's a chic shopping arcade on the ground floor, and you reach the lobby on an escalator. Public and guest rooms have been refreshed with green and russet colors. Bathroom telephones and bathrobes are standard. The restaurant, at the back of the lobby, has been downgraded to a buffet breakfast room, but there is good room service and the bar serves light snacks and light meals. *Av. de la Toison d'Or 40, B1000, tel. 02/514–2200, fax 02/514–5744. 160 rooms, 10 suites. Bar, room service, exercise room, meeting rooms. AE, DC, MC, V.*

$$$$ STANHOPE. ★ This small, exclusive hotel was created out of three adjoining town houses. All the rooms and suites have high ceilings, marble bathrooms, and luxurious furniture, but each has its own name, and no two are alike. The Linley, for example, has furniture handmade by Viscount Linley, nephew of the Queen of England. You can have English-style afternoon tea (on request) in the ground-floor salon; the gastronomic Brighton restaurant, a copy of the banqueting room of the Royal Palace, serves French specialties. The bar is open to the public. *R. du Commerce 9, B1000, tel. 02/506–9111, fax 02/512–1708. 25 rooms, 25 suites. Restaurant, bar, sauna, health club, meeting rooms, parking (fee). AE, DC, MC, V. www.summithotels.com*

$$$ BEAU-SITE. Gleaming white and with flower boxes suspended from the windowsills, this former office building makes a smart impression. The location, a block from the city-center end of Avenue Louise, and the attentive staff are big pluses. The good-size rooms come in shapes other than the standard cube, and bathrooms have hair dryers and bidets. *R. de la Longue Haie 76, B1000, tel. 02/640–8889, fax 02/640–1611. 38 rooms. In-room safes, minibars, parking (fee). AE, DC, MC, V.*

$$$ JOLLY GRAND SABLON. With an enviable position among the Sablon antiques and fine art shops, pavement cafés, and chocolate makers, the Jolly offers discreet luxury behind an elegant white facade. Its reception area, set within a hushed arcade of private art galleries, is decorated in warm russet and apricot marble. The restaurant serves Italian specialties and Sunday brunch, and looks out over a narrow alley and a pretty interior cobbled courtyard surrounded by lovingly restored redbrick houses. Rooms are decorated in pink and grey and, though some bathrooms only have showers, all include bathrobes. Suites are on the opulent side, with peach taffeta upholstery and a wall mirror that swivels round to reveal the TV. Ask for a room at the back, as the square outside is often clogged with traffic and the weekend antiques market gets going at 6 AM. *R. Bodenbroeck 2-4, B1000, tel. 02/512–8800, fax 02/512–6766. 201 rooms, 13 suites. Restaurant, bar, meeting rooms, parking (fee). AE, DC, MC, V.*

$$$ PRESIDENT CENTRE. One of three President hotels in Brussels, the Centre offers a friendly welcome in an eight-story block along the road from the Parc de Bruxelles and near the Jardin Botanique. There's a small bar at the front of the hotel and breakfast is served is a long, bright room with greenery and white tablecloths. Room service provides snacks and light meals. Furnishings are not the most modern (squashy beige plastic sofas, flowery wallpaper in bathrooms), but are in good order. Clients can use the gym and swimming pool at the President hotel near the Gare du Nord. *R. Royale 160, B1000, tel. 02/219–0065, fax 02/218–0910. 73 rooms, 5 suites. Bar, breakfast room, room service, parking (fee). AE, DC, MC, V.*

$$$ ROYAL CROWN GRAND MERCURE. With all the services of a luxury hotel, this lodging has a friendly reception staff that promises to fulfill your wishes. Rooms in the modern, eight-story building are spacious and fully air-conditioned; all are done in smart honey, green, or pink shades. Rooms on the side overlook the Jardin Botanique. *R. Royale 250, B1000, tel. 02/220–6611, fax 02/217–8444. 315 rooms, 2 suites. Bar, restaurant, no-smoking floor, exercise room, sauna, solarium, meeting rooms, parking (fee). AE, DC, MC, V.*

$$$ SCANDIC GRAND'PLACE. As its name implies, this Swedish-owned hotel near the chic Galeries St-Hubert shopping arcade is Scandinavian in inspiration and bright and efficient in manner. The reception area and bar-restaurant sit beneath a lofty atrium, and some rooms look out onto this, their window boxes filled with imitation ivy. Rooms are a little pokey and some beds are small for doubles, but there are glossy wood fittings throughout and modem connections in each. One room is specially designed for wheelchair access, several have parquet flooring to suit allergy sufferers, and some have balconies overlooking the street. The tinted windows give the impression that the weather's even greyer than it usually is outside, but their soundproofing qualities are welcome. *R. d'Arenberg, 18, B1000, tel. 02/548–1811, fax 02/548–1820. 100 rooms. Bar, restaurant, in-room data ports, 2 saunas, 6 meeting rooms. AE, DC, MC, V. www.scandicgrandplace-brussels.be*

$$ ALFA SABLON. On a quiet street between the Sablon and the Grand'Place, this hotel offers spacious rooms at an attractive price and is free of the corporate feel common to many Brussels hotels. Some rooms are on the dark side, though all have bathrooms, TV, a trouser press, and a minibar. Suites arranged in duplex style favor comfort over corporate entertainment, with a gingham-covered sofa, a spiral staircase leading up to a tiny landing and a modern classic-style bedroom in cherry wood and cream. Top-floor rooms have sloping ceilings. The basement breakfast room is rustic Mediterranean in shades of blue and yellow. *R. de la Paille, B1000, tel. 02/513–6040, fax 02/511–8141. 32 rooms, 4 suites. Bar, minibars, sauna. AE, DC, MC, V.*

$$ MANOS STÉPHANIE. The marble lobby, antiques, and Louis XV
★ furniture set a standard of elegance seldom encountered in a hotel in this price category. The rooms have rust-color carpets, green bedspreads, and good-size sitting areas. The hotel occupies a grand town house, so the rooms are not rigidly standardized. The hotel's older brother (**Manos**, Chaussée de Charleroi 100–104, tel. 02/537–9682, fax 02/539–3655) is due to reopen in 2001 with a pool and restaurant. *Chaussée de Charleroi 28, B1060, tel. 02/539–0250, fax 02/537–5729. 48 rooms, 7 suites. Bar, room service, meeting rooms, parking (fee). AE, DC, MC, V. www.manoshotel.com*

$ LES BLUETS. The floral-bedecked facade gives you an idea of
★ what to expect inside. The family that runs this no-smoking hotel

has filled their town house with all sorts of antiques and curios, including an English grandfather clock, an ecclesiastical tile mural from Colombia, and a screeching exotic bird. Every room is different—styles range from tastefully old-world to cluttered and kitschy—but all make you feel like a visitor in a much-loved house. The mother can be fearsome, especially if you don't respect the silence rule, but an authentic stay is guaranteed. There's tea and coffee in each room; some have bathrooms, some small shower units. A copious breakfast is served. *R. Berckmans 124, B1060, tel. 02/534–3983, fax 02/543–0970. 10 rooms, 1 suite. Breakfast room. AE, MC, V.*

$ SUN. Rooms are on the small side and the bathrooms are cramped, but the beds have firm mattresses and decor is a pleasant pastel green. The attractive breakfast room has a striking glass mural; snacks are served around the clock. The hotel is on a quiet but slightly dilapidated side street off the busy Chaussée d'Ixelles. *R. du Berger 38, B1050, tel. 02/511–2119, fax 02/512–3271. 22 rooms with bath or shower. Parking (fee). AE, DC, MC, V.*

CINQUANTENAIRE AND SCHUMAN

$$$$ DORINT. About as close as Brussels gets to a designer hotel, the Dorint is inspired by contemporary photography. Each room is decorated with works of a different photographer, and the navy, black, and dark-wood furnishings are sober and smart. Attention to perspective and style are evident in the chrome, black marble, and spotlights around the hotel: the circular reception area looks along a gangway to the circular restaurant, where traditional Mediterranean fare is served, but arresting artwork and greenery save it from appearing over-clinical. The green mosaic-tiled sauna, hammam, spa, and fitness center are inviting, but admission isn't included in the price. Neither is breakfast, but there's a café on site. *Bd. Charlemagne 11-19, B1000, tel. 02/231–0909, fax 02/230–3371. 210 rooms, 2 suites. Restaurant, bar, in-room data ports, in-room*

safes, sauna, spa, health club, meeting rooms, parking (fee). AE, DC, MC,
V. www.sofitel.com

$$$$ MONTGOMERY. The owners of this hotel set out to create new
standards of service for the business traveler—and, for the most
part, they have succeeded. Fax machines, three telephones (with
a private line for incoming calls), good working desks, safes, triple-
glazed windows, and bathrobes are standard. Rooms are decorated
in Chinese; English cozy; or cool, clean colonial style. There's a library
and a bar-restaurant with a wood-burning fireplace. The small
meeting rooms are well appointed. The location is conveniently
close to the European Commission. *Av. de Tervuren 134, B1150, tel.
02/741–8511, fax 02/741–8500. 61 rooms, 2 penthouses, 1 suite. Restaurant,
bar, in-room data ports, in-room safes, health club, library, meeting rooms,
parking (fee). AE, DC, MC, V. www.montgomery.be*

$$$$ SWISSÒTEL. Contemporary luxury in classic style is the flavor of
this addition to the Brussels hotel scene. Completely renovated
on its 1997 acquisition by Swissair, it is close to the European
Parliament and is a bustling hub for international lobbyists,
businesspeople, and politicians. Rooms, half of which are no-
smoking, are divided into standard and business; the latter have
large desk, espresso machines, free access to a business center
with boardroom and a club lounge, and a superior breakfast
menu. The independently run health club has a pool, Jacuzzi,
children's play area, extensive gym, aerobics classes, and beauty
treatments. Rooms at the back overlook a shared garden; all
have two phone lines and voice mail, and ISDN on demand.
Apartments, including two duplexes, can be rented for a week or
more. The hotel's Nico Central restaurant is the Brussels outpost
of Britain's gastronomic chain and offers contemporary cuisine
in a comfortable setting with yellow and blue armchairs. *R. du
Parnasse 19, B1050, tel. 02/505–2929, fax 02/505–2555. 244 rooms,
19 suites, 57 apartments. Bar, restaurant, in-room safes, no-smoking floors,
pool, beauty salon, aerobics, health club, playground, business services,
meeting rooms, parking (fee). AE, DC, MC, V. www.swissotel.com*

\$\$\$ PARK. Opposite the tall trees of the Cinquantenaire Park and with a view over their tops to the museum's glass roof, the Park Hotel offers a rare patch of green in the city's hotel spectrum. As well as the view, the grand old house has a large garden where guests can hold barbecues during the summer. The lobby with tiny bar at the end of the reception desk is colonial in style, with pillars, potted palms, and a bust of Henry Morton Stanley, who was dispatched by King Leopold II to explore the Congo. Rooms vary in size from enormous to standard; the breakfast room, which serves an English buffet breakfast, extends under a glass roof conservatory-style and overlooks the garden. The fitness center at the back of the house is small but inviting. *Av. de l'Yser 21, B1040, tel. 02/735–7400, fax 02/735–1967. 51 rooms, 1 suite. Bar, exercise room, sauna, spa, meeting rooms. AE, DC, MC, V. www.bestwestern.com*

\$\$ LEOPOLD. A discreet establishment near the European Parliament, the 10-year-old, privately owned Leopold has smallish rooms decorated in pink and grey. Bathrooms have either bath or shower. The honey-colored gastronomic restaurant has high, corniced ceilings; this is where the annual Silver Whisk competition of European hotel schools is held. There is also a pasta bar and a lunchtime brasserie; the interior courtyard is used by all three restaurants in fine weather. The solarium is a pleasant place to relax after a meal. *R. du Luxembourg 35, B1050, tel. 02/511–1828, fax 02/514–1939. 82 rooms, 4 suites, 6 apartments. 3 restaurants, bar, sauna, parking (fee). AE, DC, MC, V. www.hotel-leopold.be*

SOUTH OF CENTER

\$\$\$\$ CHÂTEAU DU LAC. Half an hour from the city center and a good
★ choice as a peaceful base from which to visit the capital and the provinces, this mock-Florentine castle is a former Schweppes bottling plant. In the late 1990s the hotel expanded to make room for more luxurious green-and-white rooms. The older, light-beige rooms are equally well furnished; the decor in the public rooms is contemporary, mostly green and wine red. The splendid

gastronomic restaurant, Le Trèfle à Quatre, serves classic French cuisine and is itself worth a visit, not only for its superb fish and game, but also for the views over the lake. *Av. du Lac 87, B1332 Genval, tel. 02/654–1122, fax 02/655–7444. 119 rooms, 2 suites. Restaurant, bar, pool, sauna, health club, convention center. AE, DC, MC, V.* cdlmartins-hotels.com

$$$ ALFA LOUISE. Located on the prestigious Avenue Louise, this hotel is distinguished by its large rooms with sitting areas and office-size desks, making it an excellent choice for budget-minded business travelers. Bathrobes and room safes are additional conveniences. *Av. Louise 212, B1000, tel. 02/644–2929, fax 02/644–1878. 43 rooms. Bar, meeting rooms. AE, DC, MC, V.*

$$$ FOUR POINTS. The concept of this Sheraton property is to offer superior rooms with limited services at moderate rates. Large rooms feature blond-wood furniture, a reclining chair, and good work space. There is a beige-and-green atrium bar, and the restaurant serves generous breakfasts and a limited selection of specialties for lunch and dinner. The basement restaurant has a separate entrance. *R. Paul Spaak 15, B1000, tel. 02/645–6111, fax 02/646–6344. 128 rooms. 2 restaurants, bar, sauna, health club, meeting rooms, parking (fee). AE, DC, MC, V.* www.fourpoints.com

$$ LES TOURELLES. This cheerful, family-run hotel is south of central Brussels but well connected by tram and street networks. The mock-medieval turreted facade and traditional wood decor suggest an antique hunting lodge, with comfortable rooms and friendly service. Try to get a back-facing room as the front looks out over a main road. *Av. Winston Churchill 135, B1180, tel. 02/344–9573, fax 02/346–4270. 22 rooms. 2 conference rooms, parking. AE, MC, V.*

WEST OF CENTER

$$ **GERFAUT.** Reasonably sized rooms in this cheerful hotel are done in light beige with colorful spreads. Those with three and four beds are available at modest supplements. Breakfast is served in the bright and friendly Winter Garden room. The location in Anderlecht near the Gare du Midi (South Station), though not choice, provides an opportunity to see a part of Brussels most visitors ignore. *Chaussée de Mons 115–117, B1070, tel. 02/524–2044, fax 02/524–3044. 48 rooms. Bar, breakfast room, free parking. AE, DC, MC, V. www.hotelgerfaut.com*

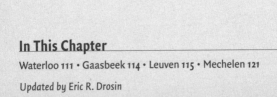

In This Chapter

Updated by Eric R. Drosin

side trips

THE REGION SURROUNDING BRUSSELS has a delightful atmosphere of historic interest and rural calm. Wellington's Headquarters stand near the battlefield at Waterloo, most of which remains as it was that fateful day in 1815. In Gaasbeek one of Belgium's most beautiful châteaux is set within a landscape that inspired the great Bruegel. Mechelen (Malines in French), north of Brussels, is a small, peaceful gem that has preserved its medieval and Renaissance past but is never overrun with tourists. The capital and social center of the province of Flemish Brabant is Leuven, the home of Belgium's oldest and most esteemed university (though, typically, the French-speaking faction of the school broke off in the 1960s and transplanted itself in Wallonian soil). The city and the province as a whole are steeped in Flemish pride, which at times can carry with it an air of disdain for Brussels, Leuven's centuries-old rival.

WATERLOO

19 km (12 mi) south of Brussels.

Waterloo, like Stalingrad or Hiroshima, changed the course of history. There are numerous Waterloos scattered across the world, but this site 19 km (11 mi) south of Brussels is the original. As Brussels spreads south, Waterloo appears to be a prosperous suburb, complete with large, whitewashed villas and smart boutiques, rather than a separate town. Home to two American international schools, it has a cosmopolitan feel to it. More than one fifth of the population is foreign, much of it American, French, and Canadian.

Sights to See

The Duke of Wellington spent the night of June 17, 1815, at an inn in Waterloo, where he established his headquarters. When he slept here again the following night, Napoléon had been defeated. The inn in the center of this pleasant, small town is now the **Musée Wellington** (Wellington Museum). It presents the events of the 100 days leading up to the Battle of Waterloo, maps and models of the battle itself, and military and Wellington memorabilia in well laid-out displays. *Chaussée de Bruxelles 147, tel. 02/354–7806. BF100/€2.50. Apr.–Oct., daily 9:30–6:30; Nov.–Mar., daily 10:30–5.*

The actual **Champ de Bataille** (battlefield) is just south of Waterloo (signposted "Butte de Lion"). This is where Wellington's troops received the onslaught of Napoléon's army. A crucial role in the battle was played by some of the ancient, fortified farms, of which there are many in this area. The farm of Hogoumont was fought over all day; 6,000 men, out of total casualties of 48,000, were killed here. Later in the day, fierce fighting raged around the farms of La Sainte Haye and Papelotte. In the afternoon, the French cavalry attacked, in the mistaken belief that the British line was giving way. Napoléon's final attempt was to send in the armored cavalry of the Imperial Guard, but at the same time the Prussian army under Blücher arrived to engage the French from the east, and it was all over. The battlefield is best surveyed from the top of the **Butte de Lion,** a pyramid 226 steps high and crowned by a 28-ton lion, which was erected by the Dutch 10 years later.

The visitor facilities at the battlefield were below par for many years, and some of the tackiness remains, including some overpriced restaurants and a seedy wax museum. The smart **visitor center** is an improvement, offering an audiovisual presentation of the battle, followed by a mood-setting film of the fighting seen through the eyes of children. You can buy souvenirs here, too—from tin soldiers and T-shirts to soft toy lions and model cannons. There are also plenty of books, some highly specialized, about the battle and the men who led the fighting. The adjacent **Battle Panorama Museum,** first unveiled in 1912, contains a vast, circular painting of the charge of the French cavalry, executed with amazing perspective and realism. *Rte. du Lion 252–254, tel. 02/385–1912. BF300/€7.40, including Butte du Lion and Panorama, BF40 just for Butte du Lion. Apr.– Sept., daily 9:30–6:30; Oct., daily 9:30–5:30; Nov.–Feb., daily 10:30– 4; Mar., daily 10–5.*

From the prevalence of souvenirs and images of Napoléon, you might think that the battle was won by the French. In fact, there were Belgian soldiers fighting on both sides. Napoléon's headquarters during his last days as emperor were in what is now the small **Musée du Caillou** in Genappe, south of the battlefield. It contains the room where he spent the night before the battle, his personal effects, and objects found in the field. *Chaussée de Bruxelles 66, tel. 02/384–2424. BF60/€1.50. Apr.–Sept., daily 10:30–6:30; Nov.–Mar., daily 1–5.*

Where to Stay and Eat

$$$ LA MAISON DU SEIGNEUR. In a peaceful, whitewashed farmhouse with a spacious terrace, Ghislaine de Becker and his son Pilou offer elegant, classical French cuisine. The menu, which changes with the seasons, includes sole with shrimp sauce and veal cooked in Porto and roast cherries. *Chaussée de Tervuren 389, tel. 02/354– 0750. AE, DC, MC, V. Closed Mon.–Tues., Feb., and 2nd ½ of Aug.*

$$ L'AUBERGE D'OHAIN. This country inn northeast of Waterloo
★ has an elegant dining room decorated in shades of peach and champagne, and a kitchen capable of great things: tagliatelle with langoustine and salmon, roast pigeon, and langoustine ravioli. The four-course *menu découverte* (tasting menu) is an excellent value. *Chaussée de Louvain 709, tel. 02/653–6497. AE, DC, MC, V. Closed Sun.–Mon. and 2nd ½ of July.*

$$ LE 1815. This small hotel is actually on the battlefield. Each room is named for one of the participating generals and decorated with his portrait. The style is art deco, but with details evocative of the period of the battle, and there is even a miniature golf course modeled after the battle. The restaurant is much better than those clustered at the foot of the Butte du Lion. *Rte. du Lion 367, B1410, tel. 02/387–0060, fax 02/387–1292. 14 rooms. Restaurant, bar, miniature golf. AE, DC, MC, V.*

$ L'AMUSOIR. Popular with resident Americans, this is an unpretentious steak house in an old white-walled building in the center of town. It serves excellent filet mignon, prepared with a variety of sauces, and hearty Belgian traditional dishes. *Chaussée de Bruxelles 121, tel. 02/353–0336. AE.*

GAASBEEK
15 km (9 mi) west of Brussels.

In Gaasbeek you are in Bruegel country, almost as if you had stepped inside one of his paintings of village life. The area is called Pajottenland, and you may be familiar with the landscape from Bruegel's works, many of which were painted here. From the terrace of the **Gaasbeek Château** you have a panoramic view of this landscape. The rulers of Gaasbeek once lorded it over Brussels, and the townspeople took terrible revenge and razed the castle. Restored in the 19th century, it contains outstanding 15th- and 16th-century tapestries. Rubens's will is among the documents in the castle archives. The surrounding park is popular with picnickers. *Kasteelstraat 40, tel. 02/532–4372. BF150/€3.70. Apr.–June and Sept.–Oct., Tues.–Thurs. and weekends 10–5; July–Aug., Sat.–Thurs. 10–5.*

En Route Beersel is just off the motorway as you head south from Brussels. It is the site of a stark, moat-surrounded, 13th-century fort, the **Kastel van Beersel,** which was part of Brussels's defenses. The interiors are empty except for one room: a well-equipped torture chamber. *Lotsestraat 65, tel. 02/331–0024. BF100/€2.50. Nov. 2–Apr. and July–Aug., Tues.–Thurs. and weekends 10–5.*

LEUVEN

26 km (16 mi) east of Brussels via the E40 or E314 autoroute.

Leuven (Louvain), like Oxford or Cambridge, is a place where underneath the hubbub of daily life you sense an age-old devotion to learning and scholarship. Its ancient Roman Catholic university, founded in 1425, was one of Europe's great seats of learning during the late Middle Ages. One of its rectors was elected Pope Adrian VI. Erasmus taught here in the 16th century, as did the cartographer Mercator and, in the following century, Cornelius Jansen, whose teachings inspired the anti-Jesuit Jansenist movement. The city was pillaged and burned by the Germans in 1914, with 1,800 buildings, including the university library, destroyed; in 1944 it was bombed again. In the 1960s, severe intercultural tensions caused the old bilingual university to split into separate French-language and Dutch-language schools. The French speakers moved their university south of the linguistic border to the new town of Louvain-la-Neuve; the Dutch-speakers remained in Leuven. Present-day **Katholieke Universiteit Leuven** has a student body of more than 25,000, including about 1,000 seminarians from many different countries.

Sights to See

★ ❶ Every Flemish town prides itself on its ornate, medieval **Stadhuis** (Town Hall). This one escaped the fires of the invading Germans in 1914 because it was occupied by German staff. It is the work of Leuven's own architectural master of Flamboyant Gothic, Mathieu de Layens, who finished it in 1469 after 21 years' work. In photographs it looks more like a finely chiseled reliquary than a building; it's necessary to stand back from it to appreciate fully the vertical lines in the mass of turrets, pinnacles, pendants, and

leuven

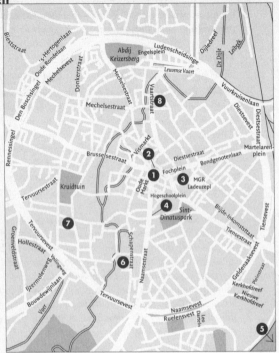

niches, each with its own statue. The interior contains some fine 16th-century sculpted ceilings. Tours are given in Flemish and English. *Grote Markt. BF50/€1.24. Tours weekdays 11 and 3, weekends 3.*

NEED A
BREAK? **Gambrinus,** on the corner of the busy Grote Markt, serves tasty sandwiches either on a terrace with a view of the Stadhuis or inside amid fin de siècle decor. *Grote Markt 13, tel. 016/20–12–38.*

❷ **Sint-Pieterskerk** (Collegiate Church of St. Peter) has had a troubled architectural history. A shifting foundation led to the shortening of the tower in the 17th century and to the replacement of the spire with a cupola in the 18th. The interior, however, is remarkable for the purity of the Gothic nave. The ambulatory and choir are closed for restoration, but some treasures usually found there, including *The Last Supper,* by Leuven's 15th-century official painter Dirk Bouts, are on temporary display in the nave. *Grote Markt. Church and Stedelijk Museum (☞ below), BF200/€4.96. Tues.–Sat. 10–5, Sun. 2–5; mid-Mar.–mid-Oct., also Mon. 10–5.*

❸ The **Stedelijk Museum Vander Kelen-Mertens** (Municipal Museum) gives you an idea of how Leuven's upper crust lived 100 years ago. The building, which dates from the 16th century, was originally a college. It became the mayor's residence in the 19th century. A series of rooms in different styles reflect his taste. The art collection includes works by Albrecht Bouts (died 1549), son of Dirk, and Quentin Metsys (1466–1530), a remarkable portraitist, as well as Brabantine sculptures from the 15th and 16th centuries. *Savoyestraat 6, tel. 016/22–69–06. Museum and St-Pieterskerk (☞ above), BF200/€4.96. Tues.–Sat. 10–5, Sun. 2–5; mid-Mar.–mid-Oct., also Mon. 10–5.*

❹ **Sint-Michielskerk** (Saint Michael's Church), designed by Jesuit architect Willem Hesius and built between 1650 and 1670, has a Baroque facade of great detail and extravagance. The ornate craftsmanship was intended to fill churchgoers with a sense of God's grandeur, and viewers today may feel a similar sense of awe. An exhibit on the church's long history lies inside. *Naamsestraat, tel. 016/23–12–45. Apr.–Sept., Tues.–Sun. 10–4.*

⑤ Abdij Van Park (Abbey of the Park) is located slightly southeast of Leuven. This 12th-century abbey is surrounded by a water mill, a massive tithe barn—where citizens used to come to donate a tenth of their annual income to the abbey and its residents—and a series of walls and archways. The abbey itself was reconstructed in the 16th and 17th centuries and bears the imprints of various architectural styles, from Romanesque to Gothic to Baroque. Of particular note are the intricate stucco ceilings in the refectory and library, two of just a handful of rooms that are open to the public. But a visit to Abdij van Park is about more than just architecture: there's an air of serenity to the entire complex that may be its greatest pleasure. *Abdijdreef 7, tel. 016/40–36–40; 016/40–63–29 for group visits. BF100/€2.48. Sun. and public holidays, tour begins at 4; groups by appointment.*

Every Flemish city worth its salt has a *begijnhof*, a city within a city, formerly inhabited by members of a Christian sisterhood dating from the 13th century. The original members were widows of fallen Crusaders. Leuven's **Groot Begijnhof** is the largest in the country. The quiet retreat numbers 72 tiny, whitewashed houses, with religious statues in small niches, dating mostly from the 17th century, grouped around the early Gothic Church of St. John the Baptist, not far from several university colleges. The carefully restored houses are inhabited by students and university staff. *Tervuursevest; from Grote Markt take Naamsestraat to Karmelletenberg and across Schapenstraat.*

⑦ Kruidtuin Hortus, created in 1738, is the oldest botanical garden in Belgium—the name translates simply as "Botanical Garden." It was created to supply medicinal plants to the university, but over time its scope expanded to include rare plants and a host of tree and shrub varieties. The 5½-acre complex includes a vast greenhouse, where you'll find a collection of tropical and subtropical plants. Needless to say, it's best to visit in the spring or summer. *Kapucijnenvoer 30, tel. 016/29–44–88. May–Sept., daily 8–8; Oct.–Apr., daily 8–5. www.leuven.be*

Leuven is considered the beer capital of Belgium, and Stella Artois the premier institution of Belgian brewing. The **Stella Artois brewery** is a mammoth building with a sleek, modern exterior. Despite the contemporary facilities, beer has been made here since 1366, originally going by the name Den Horen (The Horn). Master brewer Sebastien Artois took over the operation in 1717, and the barley beer Stella Artois was launched in 1926. Now you can marvel at the sheer enormity of the modern vats as a tour takes you through the entire brewing process. Call ahead to sign up for the tour, which is given in both Flemish and English twice daily during the week, depending on demand. *Vaartstraat 94–96, tel. 016/24–71–11. BF120/€2.97 for tour. By appointment only, weekdays 1:30 and 3.*

Where to Stay and Eat

$$$ BELLE EPOQUE. This grand town house by the station offers the most lavish dining in Leuven, served with considerable pomp in an art nouveau setting. Try lobster salad with apple, langoustines with caviar, or Bresse pigeon with truffle sauce. There's also a pleasant terrace. *Bondgenotenlaan 94, tel. 016/22–33–89. Reservations essential. AE, DC, MC, V. Closed Sun.–Mon. and 3 wks in July–Aug.*

$$$ HOLIDAY INN GARDEN COURT. The Leuven version of the ubiquitous hotel chain is conveniently located a few minutes' walk from the Grote Markt. The clean, bland accommodations are precisely what you'd expect them to be. *Alfons Smetsplein 7, tel. 016/ 31–76–00, fax 016/31–76–01. 100 rooms. Restaurant, bar, parking. AE, DC, MC, V. www.holiday-inn.com*

$$ DE BLAUWE ZON. This trendy restaurant has a mezzanine and large dining room decorated to resemble a garden. A young crowd dominates the scene; they come for Asian-Continental fusion cuisine, including such dishes as a shrimp tartare with cucumber sauce and eel and shrimp casserole. *Tiensestraat 28, tel. 016/22–68–80. V. Closed Sun., no lunch Sat.*

$$ JACKSON'S HOTEL. In a modern building opposite the hospital—where you can park for free on the weekends—and a five-minute walk from the town center, Jackson's is pleasant, modest lodging for the budget-minded. You'll find charming owners, a quiet environment, and simple, comfortable rooms (with floral-pattern curtains and bedspreads that may not be to everyone's taste). *Brusselsestraat 110-112, tel. 016/20–24–92, fax 016/23–13–29. 14 rooms. Bar. AE, DC, MC, V.*

$ DE NACHTUIL. Given the name (which translates as "The Night Owl"), it should come as no surprise that this establishment's hours of operation are 6 PM to 6 AM. The menu features fresh, simple, traditional cuisine, with an emphasis on meat dishes. The three dining halls don't score points for their standard brasserie decor, but the varied clientele gives the place a pleasantly relaxed feel. *Krakenstraat 8, tel. 016/22–02–59. No credit cards. No lunch.*

$ DOMUS. Tucked into a back street off the Grote Markt, this café adjoins the tiny Domus brewery, famous for its honey beer. The ambience is casual, the clientele on the young side, and the decor authentically rustic: craggy old beams, a brick fireplace, a labyrinth of separate rooms, bric-a-brac, and paisley table throws. The Burgundian menu includes traditional dishes such as black-and-white pudding with apples. *Tiensestraat 8, tel. 016/20–14–49. No credit cards.*

$ HOTEL PROFESSOR. Of the eight immaculate rooms here, three have a terrific view of the Oude Markt, and the price is a bargain for such a prime location. There's a wonderful café on the ground floor of the early 20th-century building. *Naamsestraat 20 , tel. 016/20–14–14, fax 016/29–14–16. 8 rooms. Bar, café. AE, DC, MC, V.*

Nightlife

The intimate **De Blauwe Kater** is one of the only bars in Leuven where you can enjoy free jazz and blues shows. Small bands perform live from October through May, usually on Wednesday and Thursday. When the place isn't swinging, you can sit back and sip a drink by candlelight. And the place doesn't close until the last customer decides to leave. *Hallengang 1, tel. 016/20–80–90. No credit cards. 7–close.*

MECHELEN

28 km (17 mi) north of Brussels, via the E19 autoroute.

As the residence of the Roman Catholic Primate of Belgium, Mechelen is an important ecclesiastical center. It's a center of vegetable production as well; the town and its environs are known for asparagus, whose stalks reach their height of perfection in May, and *witloof*, the Belgian delicacy known elsewhere as chicory or endive.

Mechelen's brief period of grandeur coincided with the reign (1507–30) of Margaret of Austria. She established her devout and cultured court in this city while she served as regent for her nephew, who later became Emperor Charles V. The philosophers Erasmus and Sir Thomas More were among her visitors, as were the painters Albrecht Dürer and Van Orley (whose portrait of Margaret hangs in the Musée d'Art Ancien in Brussels), and Josquin des Prés, the master of polyphony.

Sights to See

★ ❾ **Sint-Romboutskathedraal** (St. Rombout's Cathedral), completed in the 1520s, represents a magnificent achievement by three generations of the Keldermans family of architects, who were active

mechelen

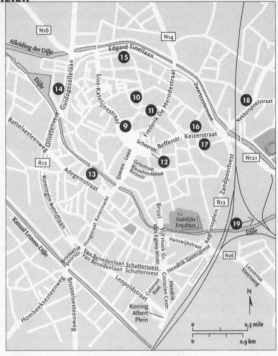

in cathedral building throughout Flanders. The beautifully proportioned tower, 318 ft high, was intended to be the tallest in the world, but the builders ran out of money before they could reach their goal. Inside are two remarkable 40-ton carillons of 49 bells each; carillon-playing was virtually invented in Mechelen (the Russian word for carillon means "sound of Mechelen"), and student carillonneurs come here from all over the world. The town's carillon school, the oldest in the world, was founded in 1923. The best place to listen to the bells is in the Minderbroedersgang. The interior of the cathedral is spacious and lofty, particularly the white sandstone nave dating from the 13th century. Chief among the art treasures is Van Dyck's *Crucifixion* in the south transept. *Grote Markt. Mon.–Sat. 9–4 (until 6 in summer), Sun. 1–5; check tourist office for tower tours; carillon concerts Sat. 11:30 AM, Sun. 3, Mon. 8:30 PM.*

12 Seldom have two parts of a single building had such vividly contrasting styles as do those of Mechelen's **Stadhuis** (Town Hall). To the right is the Gothic, turreted, 14th-century *Lakenhalle* (Cloth Hall). To the left is the flamboyant palace commissioned by Charles V to accommodate the *Grote Raad* (Grand Council) of the Burgundian Netherlands. Work was abandoned in 1547 but resumed and completed in the 20th century in accordance with the original plans of the Keldermans, Mechelen's first family of architects. *Grote Markt. Guided tours (from tourist office), Easter–June and Sept., weekends 2; July–Aug., daily 2.*

NEED A BREAK? The smallest café in Mechelen is the **Borrel Babel** in the charming Sint-Romboutshof, behind the cathedral. Different varieties of jenever (Dutch gin) are the potent specialty.

13 By the old **Haverwerf** (Oat Wharf, where oats once were loaded) and near the **Zoutwerf** (Salt Wharf), both on the river Dijle, you'll find three remarkable houses, side by side. The green **Het Paradijs** (Paradise) is Gothic, with a relief showing the banishment of

124

Adam and Eve. Next to it stands the **Duivelsgevel** (Little Devils), with a 15th-century timber facade decorated with carved satyrs. The third of the group is the red **Sint Josef,** a Baroque house from 1669. Also worth note, on the Zoutwerf, is the old **fishmongers' guildhall.** It dates from the 16th century and is embellished by a magnificent golden salmon. *Haverwerf.*

⑭ Het Anker (The Anchor) is the birthplace of Mechelen's pride and joy, the dark, sweet Gouden Carolus (Golden Charles) beer. Touring this small, intimate brewery, you can witness every stage of the beer-making process. (Tours in English must be arranged in advance.) Devoted beer fans can spend the night—a modest 22-room hotel is part of the brewery complex. *Guido Gezellelaan 49, tel. 015/20–38–80. BF125/€3.10. June–Aug., daily 10:30–6, guided tours at 3.*

⑮ Belgium's Shoah museum, **Museum van Deportatie en Verzet** (The Museum of Deportation and the Resistance), is built in a wing of the former Gen. Dossin de Saint-Georges barracks, used by the Nazis as the starting point for the deportation of some 25,257 prisoners from Mechelen to Auschwitz. The museum's exhibits tell the story of the deportation and extermination of almost half of Belgium's Jewish population during World War II. You'll also find information about the resistance movement, a history of antisemitism, and a chronology of Jewish life in Belgium and Europe. *Goswin de Stassartstraat 153, tel. 015/29–06–60. Sun.–Thurs. 10–5, Fri. 10–1. www2.cipal.be/cicb*

⑯ The **Koninklijke Manufactuur Gaspard De Wit** (Royal Tapestry Factory) is a great place to learn about different styles of tapestry weaving, and one of the few places where this ancient and glorious art is still practiced. Tours of the workshops permit you to watch the experts creating new pieces and restoring old ones, and there's a collection of antique and contemporary tapestries on display. Official opening hours are severely restricted, but see what the Tourist Office can do for you at other times. *Schoutetstraat 7,* *tel. 015/20–29–05. Guided tours, BF200/€4.96. Guided tours, Aug.–June, Sat. 10:30.*

⑪ The 15th-century Gothic **Sint-Janskerk** (Church of Saint John) is a treasure house of religious art. Peter Paul Rubens's tryptich *The Adoration of the Magi*, works by masters such as de Crayer, van der Veken, and Valckx, and the magnificent wood carvings of the pulpit and confessionals merit several hours of your time. Although you'll find art dating from the 16th century through the 20th, the church purchased the majority of its works in the 16th and 17th centuries—a period when it had the benefit of deep coffers. Note that visits are not permitted during church services or on December 25, 26, and 31. *Sint Jansstraat, tel. 015/29–76–55. Apr.–Oct., daily 1–5; Nov.–Mar., daily noon–4.*

⑯ The **Sint-Pieter en Pauluskerk** (Church of Saint Peter and Saint Paul) lies on the corner of the *Veemarkt*, or cattle market, its construction completed by the Jesuit order in 1677. This baroque church has an astounding 14 confessionals, artfully crafted oak paneling, and a pulpit made by the sculptor Verbruggen in the early 18th century. You can also enjoy a considerable 17th-century art collection, with works by Coxie and Quellien, among others. Note that visits are not permitted during church services or on Dec. 25, 26, and 31 *Keizerstraat, tel. 015/29–76–55. Apr.–Oct., daily 1–5; Nov.–Mar., daily noon–4.*

⑰ The **Oud Paleis van Margareta van Oostenrijk** (Former Palace of Margaret of Austria) was erected in 1507, blending traditional Gothic architecture and early Renaissance design. The gatehouse, for example, designed by French architect Guy de Beaugrant, was one of the first works of the Renaissance style in northwestern Europe. Following its use as a residence by Cardinal Granvelle and as a place of work by the Great Council of the Netherlands, the palace is now the town's justice building, containing a number of courts. You aren't allowed to tour the palace itself, but you can visit the immaculately manicured interior courtyard, with its conical hedges and prim flower beds. *Keizerstraat, tel. 015/29–76–55. Weekdays 10–5.*

⑱ Speelgoedmuseum Mechelen (Mechelen Toy Museum) is one of the biggest toy museums in the world. It has more than 8,000 tin soldiers standing ready to do battle on a model of Waterloo plus a vast collection of toys and games, both ancient and modern, and a play area for young and old. A regularly rotating series of exhibitions makes this a ceaselessly fascinating place. *Nekkerspoel 21, tel. 015/55–70–75. BF180/€4.46. Tues.–Sun. 10–5.*

⑲ At **Planckendael,** more than 1,000 animals lead a life of near-freedom. The vast park has an adventure trail for children, a large playground, and a children's farm. The park can be reached by boat from Mechelen (leaving from the Colomabrug bridge), with departures every 30 minutes starting at 9 in the morning and running through the day. *Leuvensesteenweg 582, Muizen, tel. 015/41–42–49. BF460/€11.40. Jan., daily 9–4:30; Feb., mid-Oct.–Dec., daily 9–4:45; early Mar., early Oct., daily 9–5:15; late Mar.–June, Sept., daily 9–5:45; July–Aug., daily 9–6:15.*

Where to Stay and Eat

$$$ D'HOOGH. In a grand gray-stone mansion on the Grote Markt, ★ its second-floor dining room looking over the square, this glamorous landmark presents top-quality *cuisine du marché* (whatever is freshest): smoked-eel terrine with pistachios; poached goose liver in port jelly with caramelized apples; turbot and zucchini spaghetti in vinaigrette and olive oil; and, in April and May, the most wonderful asparagus imaginable. *Grote Markt 19, tel. 015/21–75–53. Reservations essential. AE, DC, MC, V. Closed Mon. and 1st 3 wks of Aug. No lunch Sat., no dinner Sun.*

$$$ HOTEL ALFA ALBA. Some five minutes' walk from the Grote Markt and right next to the Musée Michiels, the clock and bell museum, this hotel offers a chance to relax in the comfort of a traditional "English library" setting. The rooms are cozy and offer TV, a trouser press, and mini-safes. *Korenmarkt 22-26, tel. 015/42–03–03, fax 015/42–37–88. 43 rooms. Restaurant, bar, parking (fee). AE, DC, MC, V.*

$$ DE KEIZEREN. Boasting hearty fare and an even heartier crowd, this tavern-restaurant offers traditional Belgian food at relatively modest prices. The interior decor is uninspired, but the spacious outdoor terrace provides a lovely view of the Grote Markt. On the menu you'll find tasty meat *brochettes* as well as such classics as spaghetti Bolognese and steak béarnaise. *Bruul 1, tel. 015/20–66–41. MC, V.*

$$ HOTEL DEN GROOTEN WOLSACK. Located just behind the Sint-Romboutskathedraal, this renovated hotel consists of an original 15th-century building with more recent additions. The clean, adequately large rooms have a neoclassical decor, and the slightly more expensive suites look out onto the peaceful interior courtyard. *Wollemarkt 16, tel. 015/28–55–60, fax 015/21–77–81. 14 rooms. Restaurant, bar, parking (fee). AE, DC, MC, V.*

$$ HOTEL GULDEN ANKER. Open since 1987, this distinguished hotel prides itself on its terrific restaurant, which blends French and local cuisine, and its comfortable rooms. It's situated a little outside the center of town, near the Vrijbroekpark (Town Park), giving it a calm, bucolic setting. *Brusselsesteenweg 2, tel. 015/42–25–35, fax 015/42–34–99. 34 rooms. Restaurant, bar. AE, DC, MC, V. www.guldenanker.be*

$ BRASSERIE DEN BEER. In the pervasively traditional city of Mechelen, Den Beer is an oasis of modernism. The decor is dominated by glass and leather, and the elevated outdoor terrace has the requisite austere gray awning. The food is conventional Continental fare—salad Niçoise, spaghetti Bolognese, and steak with french fries are menu standards. This is a good place to try one (or more) of Mechelen's three speciality beers: Mechelschen Bruyen, Toison d'Or, and Gouden Carolus. The desserts, such as

Your checklist for a perfect journey

WAY AHEAD

- Devise a trip budget.

- Write down the five things you want most from this trip. Keep this list handy before and during your trip.

- Make plane or train reservations. Book lodging and rental cars.

- Arrange for pet care.

- Check your passport. Apply for a new one if necessary.

- Photocopy important documents and store in a safe place.

A MONTH BEFORE

- Make restaurant reservations and buy theater and concert tickets. Visit fodors.com for links to local events.

- Familiarize yourself with the local language or lingo.

TWO WEEKS BEFORE

- Replenish your supply of medications.

- Create your itinerary.

- Enjoy a book or movie set in your destination to get you in the mood.

- Develop a packing list. Shop for missing essentials. Repair and launder or dry-clean your clothes.

A WEEK BEFORE

- Stop newspaper deliveries. Pay bills.

- Acquire traveler's checks.

- Stock up on film.

- Label your luggage.

- Finalize your packing list— take less than you think you need.

- Create a toiletries kit filled with travel-size essentials.

- Get lots of sleep. Don't get sick before your trip.

A DAY BEFORE

- Drink plenty of water.

- Check your travel documents.

- Get packing!

DURING YOUR TRIP

- Keep a journal/scrapbook.

- Spend time with locals.

vanilla ice cream covered in a rich raspberry sauce, are particularly recommended. *Grote Markt 32-33, tel. 015/20–97–06. MC, V.*

$ 'T KORENVELD. This tiny, old-fashioned bistro has been primly restored and decked with pretty floral wallpaper and tile tabletops. Its cuisine is unpretentious, featuring simple fish and steaks at low prices. It adjoins the Alfa Hotel and has some tables in the hotel bar. *Korenmarkt 20, tel. 015/42–14–69. AE, MC, V. Closed Sun.–Mon. and Aug. No dinner Sat.*

PRACTICAL INFORMATION

Air Travel

Flying time to Brussels is about 7 hours from New York and 8¼ hours from Chicago. Depending upon your routing and transit time, flights from Dallas last approximately 13 hours; flights from Los Angeles, approximately 17 hours; and flights from Sydney, approximately 24 hours.

CARRIERS

When flying internationally, you must usually choose between a domestic carrier, the national flag carrier of the country, such as Sabena Airlines for Belgium, and a foreign carrier from a third country. Smaller carriers are usually inexpensive, but do not fly daily and often do not fly year-round.

American, Delta, Sabena, United, and City Bird fly into Brussels from the United States. Sabena, British Midland, and British Airways fly to Brussels from London's Heathrow Airport; Air UK from Stansted; and British Airways from Gatwick. Several regional centers in the United Kingdom also have direct flights to Brussels, as do all capitals in Europe and a growing number of secondary cities. The no-frills airline Virgin Express offers scheduled flights between London and Brussels.

➤ MAJOR AIRLINES: **Air France** (tel. 800/237–2724). **American** (tel. 800/433–7300; 02/548–2122 in Belgium). **British Airways** (tel. 800/247–99297). **British Midland** (tel. 02/771–7766). **Continental** (tel. 800/344–6888). **Delta** (tel. 800/221–1212; 02/730–8200 in Belgium). **Sabena** (tel. 800/221–4750; 02/723–2323 in Belgium). **United** (tel. 800/241–6522; 02/713–3600 in Belgium).

➤ SMALLER AIRLINES: **City Bird** (tel. 888/248–9247; 02/752–5252 in Belgium). **Canada 3000** (tel. 888/226–3000). **Virgin Express** (tel. 0207/744–0004 in the U.K.; 02/752–0505 in Belgium).

Airports & Transfers

The major airport serving Brussels is the Brussels National Airport at Zaventem. Brussels National Airport has nonstop flights from the United States and Canada, and a wide range of amenities such as airport hotels, rental car agencies, and travel agencies.

➤ **AIRPORT INFORMATION: Brussels National Airport** (tel. 02/753–3913).

TRANSFERS

Courtesy buses serve airport hotels and a few downtown hotels: inquire when making reservations. Express trains leave the airport for the Gare du Nord and Gare Centrale stations every 20 minutes (one train an hour continues to the Gare du Midi). The trip takes 20 minutes and costs BF140/€3.45 one way in first class, BF90/€2.25 second class. The trains operate 6 AM to midnight. Taxis are plentiful. A taxi to the city center takes about half an hour and costs about BF1,200/€30. You can save 25% on the fare by buying a voucher for the return trip if you use the Autolux taxi company. Beware freelance taxi drivers who hawk their services in the arrival hall.

➤ **TAXIS & SHUTTLES: Autolux** (tel. 02/411–1221).

Bike Travel

Cycling in cities is less than pleasant, as traffic is dense, bicycle paths are scarce, and city drivers are generally not as hospitable about sharing the road with cyclists.

➤ **BIKE MAPS: La Route de Jade** (116 rue de Stassart, Brussels, tel. 02/512–9654).

Bus Travel

If you're planning to travel extensively in Europe, it may make sense to invest in a Eurolines Pass for unlimited coach travel between 48 cities including Brussels. Fares and schedules are available at the Eurolines sales office or at local travel agencies. As of spring 2000, a 30-day Eurolines Pass cost $350 ($280 if you're under 26).

Eurolines offers up to three daily express bus services from Amsterdam, Berlin, Frankfurt, Paris, and London. The Eurolines Coach Station is located at CCN Gare du Nord.

From London, the City Sprint bus connects with the Dover–Calais Hovercraft, and the bus then takes you on to Brussels. For reservations and times, call Hoverspeed.

To Waterloo, Bus W from Brussels (Place Rouppe) runs at half-hour intervals.

➤ **Bus Information: CCN Gare du Nord**(R. du Progrès 80, tel. 02/203–0707). **Hoverspeed**(tel. 01304/240241). **Eurolines** (52 Grosvenor Gardens, London SW1W oAU, U.K., tel. 0171/730–8235, fax 0171/730–8721).

Business Hours

Banks in Brussels are open from 9 until 4, Monday through Friday. Small local banks close between 12:30 and 2. Office hours are generally from 9 until 6. Most offices close for lunch between 12:30 and 2, although post offices do not close for lunch. Government offices are open from 9 until 5. Gas stations are generally open from 7 AM until 7 PM. In small villages, gas stations often close on Sunday and for lunch from 12:30 until 2. Gas stations on highways do not close for lunch and are usually open until midnight.

Most museums in Brussels are closed on Monday, Christmas Day, New Years Day, All Saints Day, and Armistice Day. Museum hours are generally from 10 until 5. National museums stay open during lunchtime. Smaller private museums may close between 12:30 and 2. Most pharmacies are open until 7 on weekdays and are closed on weekends. For urgent prescriptions, closed pharmacies post signs indicating the nearest open pharmacies (*pharmaciens de guarde* in French or *dienstdoend apotekers* in Flemish).

In cities where security is a problem, rather than keep the entire shop open, pharmacists use a small window for fulfilling prescriptions at night. Except for souvenir shops in tourist areas, bakeries, and some delicatessens and flower shops, all shops are closed on Sunday. The rest of the week, shops are open from 10 until 6. Small neighborhood shops often close for lunch between 1 and 2. Bakeries, delicatessens, and other small grocery stores remain open until 7. Supermarkets are open from 9 until 8, and the larger ones remain open until 9 on Friday. Duty-free shops at Brussels National Airport are open daily from 6 AM until 9 PM.

Car Rental

The major car rental firms have booths at the airport. This is convenient, but the airport charges rental companies a fee that is passed on to customers, so you may want to rent from the downtown locations of rental firms. Consider also whether you want to get off a transatlantic flight and into an unfamiliar car in an unfamiliar city. Rental agencies are also at the Midi train station in Brussels.

Rental cars are European brands and range from economy, such as an Opel Corsa, to luxury, such as a Mercedes. It is also possible to rent minivans. Rates in Brussels vary from company to company; daily rates for budget companies start at approximately $40 for an economy car including collision insurance. This does not include mileage, airport fee, and 17½% VAT tax. Weekly rates often include unlimited mileage.

➤ MAJOR AGENCIES: **Alamo** (tel. 800/522–9696; 020/8759–6200 in the U.K.). **Avis** (tel. 800/331–1084; 800/331–1084 in Canada; 02/9353–9000 in Australia; 09/525–1982 in New Zealand; 02/730–6211 in Belgium). **Budget** (tel. 800/527–0700; 0870/607–5000 in

134

the U.K., through affiliate Europcar; 02/646–5130 in Belgium). **Dollar** (tel. 800/800–6000; 0124/622–0111 in the U.K., through affiliate Sixt Kenning; 02/9223–1444 in Australia). **Hertz** (tel. 800/654–3001; 800/263–0600 in Canada; 020/8897–2072 in the U.K.; 02/9669–2444 in Australia; 09/256–8690 in New Zealand; 2/513–2886 in Belgium). **National Car Rental** (tel. 800/227–7368; 020/8680–4800 in the U.K., where it is known as National Europe).

Car Travel

An extensive network of four-lane, well-lit, well-maintained, toll-free highways make highway travel easy in Belgium. Under good conditions, you should be able to travel on highways at an average of about 70 mi per hour. Brussels is 204 km (122 mi) from Amsterdam on E19; 222 km (138 mi) from Düsseldorf on E40; 219 km (133 mi) from Luxembourg City on E411; and 308 km (185 mi) from Paris.

If you piggyback on Le Shuttle through the Channel Tunnel, the distance is 213 km (128 mi) from Calais to Brussels; the route from Calais via Oostende is the fastest, even though on the Belgian side the highway stops a few kilometers short of the border. If you take the ferry to Oostende, the distance is 115 km (69 mi) to Brussels on the six-lane E40.

Brussels is surrounded by a beltway, marked RING. Exits to the city are marked CENTER. Among several large underground parking facilities, the one close to the Grand'Place is particularly convenient if you're staying in a downtown hotel.

EMERGENCY SERVICES

If you break down on the highway, **look for emergency telephones** located at regular intervals. The emergency telephones are connected to an emergency control room that can send a tow truck. It is also possible to take out an emergency automobile insurance that covers all of your expenses in case of a breakdown on the road.

➤ CONTACTS: **Europ Assistance** (tel. 02/533–7575). **Touring Secours** (tel. 02/233–2211).

GASOLINE
Major credit cards are widely accepted at gasoline stations throughout the country. Leaded and unleaded gas and deisel fuel are available at all stations. Costs vary between 75¢ per liter for deisel fuel and $1 per liter for unleaded gas. Drivers normally pump their own gas, but full service is available at many stations.

ROAD CONDITIONS
Rush hour traffic is worst from September until June. Peak rush hour traffic is from 7 AM to 9:30 AM and from 4 PM to 7:30 PM, Monday through Friday. You are most likely to encounter traffic jams as you travel into cities in the morning, out of cities in the afternoon, and on ring roads around major cities in the morning and in the afternoon.

City driving is challenging because of chronic double parking and lack of street-side parking. Beware of slick cobblestone streets in rainy weather.

RULES OF THE ROAD
Use of seatbelts is compulsory in Belgium, both in front and rear seats, and there are fines for disobeying. Turning right on a red light is not permitted.

In Brussels, **approach crossings with care.** Stop signs are few and far between. Instead, small triangles are painted on the road of the driver who must yield. Otherwise, priority is given to the driver coming from the right, and drivers in Belgium exercise that priority fervently.

Illegally parked cars are ticketed, and the fine is approximately $25. If you park in a tow-away zone, you risk having your car towed, paying a fee of about $100, and receiving a traffic ticket.

Cruise Travel

Belgium's rivers and canals provide an interesting perspective for sightseeing. A variety of half-day and full-day cruises are available from May to September. Reservations are required.

➤ CRUISE LINES: **Brussels by Water** (2bis, quai des Péniches, 1000, Brussels, tel. 322/203–6404). **Centraal Boekingskantoor Bootochten (CBB)** (Heilig Hartlaan 30, 9300, Aalst, tel. 3253/729–440).

Customs & Duties

When shopping, **keep receipts** for all purchases. Upon reentering the country, **be ready to show customs officials what you've bought.** If you feel a duty is incorrect or object to the way your clearance was handled, note the inspector's badge number and ask to see a supervisor. If the problem isn't resolved, write to the appropriate authorities, beginning with the port director at your point of entry.

IN AUSTRALIA

Australian residents who are 18 or older may bring home $A400 worth of souvenirs and gifts (including jewelry), 250 cigarettes or 250 grams of tobacco, and 1,125 ml of alcohol (including wine, beer, and spirits). Residents under 18 may bring back $A200 worth of goods. Prohibited items include meat products. Seeds, plants, and fruits need to be declared upon arrival.

➤ INFORMATION: **Australian Customs Service** (Regional Director, Box 8, Sydney, NSW 2001, tel. 02/9213–2000, fax 02/9213–4000).

IN BELGIUM

Americans and other non-EU members are allowed to bring in no more than 200 cigarettes, 50 cigars, 1 liter of spirits, 2 liters of wine or sparkling wine, 50 grams of perfume, and 25 liters of toilet water. EU members may bring in 800 cigarettes; 200 cigars; 10 liters of spirits; 90 liters of wine, of which 60 liters may be sparkling wine; 50 grams of perfume; and 25 liters of toilet water.

IN CANADA

Canadian residents who have been out of Canada for at least 7 days may bring home C$500 worth of goods duty-free. If you've been away less than 7 days but more than 48 hours, the duty-free allowance drops to C$200; if your trip lasts 24–48 hours, the allowance is C$50. You may not pool allowances with family members. Goods claimed under the C$500 exemption may follow you by mail; those claimed under the lesser exemptions must accompany you. Alcohol and tobacco products may be included in the 7-day and 48-hour exemptions but not in the 24-hour exemption. If you meet the age requirements of the province or territory through which you reenter Canada, you may bring in, duty-free, 1.14 liters (40 imperial ounces) of wine or liquor or 24 12-ounce cans or bottles of beer or ale. If you are 16 or older you may bring in, duty-free, 200 cigarettes and 50 cigars. Check ahead of time with Revenue Canada or the Department of Agriculture for policies regarding meat products, seeds, plants, and fruits.

You may send an unlimited number of gifts worth up to C$60 each duty-free to Canada. Label the package UNSOLICITED GIFT—VALUE UNDER $60. Alcohol and tobacco are excluded.

➤ INFORMATION: **Revenue Canada** (2265 St. Laurent Blvd. S, Ottawa, Ontario K1G 4K3, tel. 613/993–0534; 800/461–9999 in Canada, fax 613/957–8911, www.ccra-adrc.gc.ca).

IN NEW ZEALAND

Homeward-bound residents 17 or older may bring back $700 worth of souvenirs and gifts. Your duty-free allowance also includes 4.5 liters of wine or beer; one 1,125-ml bottle of spirits; and either 200 cigarettes, 250 grams of tobacco, 50 cigars, or a combination of the three up to 250 grams. Prohibited items include meat products, seeds, plants, and fruits.

➤ INFORMATION: **New Zealand Customs** (Custom House, 50 Anzac Ave., Box 29, Auckland, tel. 09/359–6655, fax 09/359–6732).

IN THE U.K.

If you are a U.K. resident and your journey was wholly within the European Union (EU), you won't have to pass through customs when you return to the United Kingdom. If you plan to bring back large quantities of alcohol or tobacco, check EU limits beforehand.

➤ INFORMATION: **HM Customs and Excise** (Dorset House, Stamford St., Bromley, Kent BR1 1XX, tel. 0171/202–4227).

IN THE U.S.

U.S. residents who have been out of the country for at least 48 hours (and who have not used the $400 allowance or any part of it in the past 30 days) may bring home $400 worth of foreign goods duty-free.

U.S. residents 21 and older may bring back 1 liter of alcohol duty-free. In addition, regardless of your age, you are allowed 200 cigarettes and 100 non-Cuban cigars. Antiques, which the U.S. Customs Service defines as objects more than 100 years old, enter duty-free, as do original works of art done entirely by hand, including paintings, drawings, and sculptures.

You may also send packages home duty-free: up to $200 worth of goods for personal use, with a limit of one parcel per addressee per day (except alcohol or tobacco products or perfume worth more than $5); label the package PERSONAL USE and attach a list of its contents and their retail value. Do not label the package UNSOLICITED GIFT or your duty-free exemption will drop to $100. Mailed items do not affect your duty-free allowance on your return.

➤ INFORMATION: **U.S. Customs Service** (1300 Pennsylvania Ave. NW, Washington, DC 20229, www.customs.gov; inquiries tel. 202/354–1000; complaints c/o Office of Regulations and Rulings; registration of equipment c/o Resource Management, tel. 202/927–0540).

Dining

Brussels offers a wide variety of restaurants ranging from snack stands, cafés, and pubs to top-rated restaurants serving gourmet cuisine. The better restaurants are on a par with the most renowned in the world. Prices ranges are similar to those in France and in Great Britain. The restaurants we list throughout this book are the cream of the crop in each price category.

Most restaurants are open for lunch and dinner only. Restaurants and hotel pension packages serve hot three-course meals including a starter or soup, a main course, and dessert. A set-price, three-course menu for lunch (*déjeuner* in French, *middagmaal* in Flemish) is offered in many restaurants. Dinner (*dîner* in French, *avondmaal* in Flemish) menus are very similar to lunch menus. Diners are not commonly given a choice of vegetables or salad dressing.

Some large hotels serve buffet breakfast (*petit déjeuner* in French, *ontbijt* in Flemish) with cooked American fare. Smaller hotels and bed-and-breakfasts serve bread, rolls, butter, jam, and cheese with juice and coffee or tea and occasionally a soft-boiled egg.

Cafés and snack bars are open in the morning and serve coffee, tea, juice, and rolls, but they do not serve a full American-style breakfast. You can also order a quick sandwich lunch or light one-course meal at cafés, pubs, cafeterias, and snack bars.

MEALS & SPECIALTIES

Most of Brussels restaurants feature Continental cuisine similar to that of France. Many restaurants also offer hearty traditional fare. During hunting season, restaurants and country inns often feature a special hunter's menu including *sanglier* (wild boar) and *faisan* (pheasant).

Moules (mussels) are one of the most ubiquitous dishes in Brussels, often served with *frites* (french fries), which Belgians proudly claim have been invented in Belgium and not in France.

Other Belgian specialties to try include *waterzooi*, a creamy chicken stew, or *carbonnades*, a beef stew cooked in beer. *Stoemp* is a filling mixture of mashed potatoes and vegetables. Belgian endive (*chicons* in French, *witloof* in Flemish) is usually cooked with ham, braised, and topped with a cheese gratin. A popular first course is tomato filled with tiny gray shrimp (*crevettes* in French, *garnaal* in Flemish), fresh from Belgium's North Sea.

MEALTIMES

Breakfast is served in hotels from about 7 to 10. Lunch is served in restaurants from noon until 2, and dinner from 7 to 9. Pubs and cafés serve snacks until midnight. Many restaurants are closed on Sunday for dinner, and restaurants in cities often close on Saturday for lunch.

Unless otherwise noted, the restaurants listed in this guide are open daily for lunch and dinner.

PAYING

Major credit cards are accepted in most restaurants in Brussels. Visa is the most widely accepted credit card. Smaller establishments occasionally do not accept American Express or Diners Club. Credit cards usually cannot be used for purchasing snacks at pubs and cafés. Do not rely on travelers checks for paying restaurant bills.

A 15% service charge is usually included in the cost of a meal. Nonetheless, it is customary to **round off the total,** adding a small amount for good service.

RESERVATIONS & DRESS

Reservations are always a good idea: we mention them only when they're essential or not accepted. Book as far ahead as you can, and confirm as soon as you arrive. We mention dress only when men are required to wear a jacket or a jacket and tie.

WINE, BEER, & SPIRITS

Belgium is a beer-lover's paradise. Artisanal breweries produce more than 400 types of beer, many of which are offered in

Belgian pubs and cafés. Kriek, a fruit-flavored beer, and Duvel, a very strong dark beer, are popular among Belgians. Some of Belgium's trappist monastaries still produce their own brews, such as Orval, Leffe, and Chimay. Popular mass-produced brands are Stella Artois and Maes.

Licenses are not required for sale of beer or wine in dining establishments. As a result, beer is served at virtually all restaurants, snack bars, pubs, and cafés, and wine is served at all restaurants and most other establishments. There is no legal minimum age for consumption of beer or wine. Sale of hard liquor does require a license, and the legal age for consumption of liquor is 18. The cost of beer and wine in dining establishments is very reasonable. Liquor and mixed cocktails are considerably more expensive.

Disabilities & Accessibility

In Brussels, hotels with facilities to accommodate guests with disabilities are identified in guides published by national and local tourist offices. Awareness of the sensitivities of people with disabilities is generally high but has not yet impacted on the language; the words *handicapé* (French) and *gehandicapt* (Dutch) are still commonly used. Visitors with disabilities should be aware that many streets in Brussels are cobblestone.

For information on facilities in Belgium, contact **Vlaamse Federatie voor Gehandicapten**. Most trains and buses have special seats for riders with disabilities, and parking lots have spaces reserved for people with disabilities.

➤ LOCAL RESOURCES: **Vlaamse Federatie voor Gehandicapten** (66 Grensstraat 1210, Brussels, tel. 02/219–8800).

LODGING

The following hotels in Brussels (listed from most expensive to least) have rooms for guests with disabilities: Conrad, Hilton, Jolly Hotel Grand Sablon, Meridien, Radisson SAS, Renaissance, Sodehotel La Woluwe, Bristol Stephanie, Sheraton Brussels,

Sheraton Brussels Airport, Arctia, Four Points, Métropole, Holiday Inn Brussels Airport, Jolly Atlanta, Mercure, Novotel Brussels (off Grand'Place), Novotel Airport, Aris, Atlas, Palace, Albert Premier, Astrid, Capital, Green Park, Fimotel Airport, Fimotel Expo, Ibis (Brussels Centre, Sainte-Catherine, and Airport), Balladins, Orion, Campanile, Comfort Inn, Gerfaut, France.

SIGHTS & ATTRACTIONS

Many, but not all, of Brussel's tourist attractions are wheelchair accessible. Belgium's tourism office (☞ Visitor Information, *below*) publishes a brochure that lists all of its attractions and museums, indicating with a wheelchair icon the attractions that are wheelchair accessible.

➤ TRAVELERS WITH MOBILITY PROBLEMS: **Access Adventures** (206 Chestnut Ridge Rd., Rochester, NY 14624, tel. 716/889–9096), run by a former physical-rehabilitation counselor. **CareVacations** (5-5110 50th Ave., Leduc, Alberta T9E 6V4, tel. 780/986–6404 or 877/478–7827, fax 780/986–8332, www.carevacations.com), for group tours and cruise vacations. **Flying Wheels Travel** (143 W. Bridge St., Box 382, Owatonna, MN 55060, tel. 507/451–5005 or 800/535–6790, fax 507/451–1685, www.flyingwheels.com).

Electricity

To use your U.S.-purchased electric-powered equipment, **bring a converter and adapter.** The electrical current in Belgium is 220 volts, 50 cycles alternating current (AC); wall outlets take Continental-type plugs, with two round prongs.

If your appliances are dual-voltage, you'll need only an adapter. Don't use 110-volt outlets marked FOR SHAVERS ONLY for high-wattage appliances such as blow-dryers. Most laptops operate equally well on 110 and 220 volts and so require only an adapter.

Embassies

➤ AUSTRALIA: **Australian Embassy to Belgium and Luxembourg** (Rue Guimard 6 8, 1000, Brussels, tel. 02/286–0500).

➤ CANADA: **Canadian Embassy to Belgium and Luxembourg** (Av. Tervueren 2, 1040, Brussels, tel. 02/741–0611).

➤ NEW ZEALAND: **New Zealand Embassy to Belgium** (Boulevard du Régent 47, 1000, Brussels, tel. 02/512–1040).

➤ REPUBLIC OF IRELAND: **Republic of Ireland Embassy to Belgium** (R. Froissart 89, tel. 02/230–5337).

➤ UNITED KINGDOM: **United Kingdom Embassy to Belgium** (Rue Arlon 85, 1040, Brussels, tel. 02/287–6232).

➤ UNITED STATES: **United States Embassy to Belgium** (Boulevard du Régent 27, 1000, Brussels, tel. 32/2–508–2111).

Emergencies

In case of medical emergencies, **dial 100** for an ambulance, which will take you to the nearest hospital or clinic's emergency center. Ambulance personnel and police in Belgium are very cooperative and can speak some English.

One pharmacy in each district stays open 24 hours; the roster is posted in all pharmacy windows. In an emergency call the pharmacy line.

➤ DOCTORS & DENTISTS: **Doctor** (tel. 02/479–1818). **Dentist** (tel. 02/426–1026).

➤ EMERGENCY SERVICES: **Police** (tel. 101). **Medical emergencies, fire, accidents, ambulance** (tel. 100). **Poison control** (tel. 070/245–245). **English-speaking help line** (tel. 02/648–4014).

➤ PHARMACIES: **Emergency pharmacy line** tel. 02/479–1818.

Gay & Lesbian Travel

Social attitudes in Belgium are tolerant toward gays, especially in bigger cities. There are several gay and lesbian organizations in Brussels.

▶ **Local Resources: English-Speaking Gay Group** (EGG; B.P. 198, 1060 Brussels). For Jewish gays and lesbians, **Shalhomo** (Av. Besme 127, 1190 Brussels, Belgium).

▶ **Gay- & Lesbian-Friendly Travel Agencies: Different Roads Travel** (8383 Wilshire Blvd., Suite 902, Beverly Hills, CA 90211, tel. 323/651–5557 or 800/429–8747, fax 323/651–3678). **Kennedy Travel** (314 Jericho Turnpike, Floral Park, NY 11001, tel. 516/352–4888 or 800/237–7433, fax 516/354–8849, www.kennedytravel.com). **Now Voyager** (4406 18th St., San Francisco, CA 94114, tel. 415/626–1169 or 800/255–6951, fax 415/626–8626, www.nowvoyager.com). **Skylink Travel and Tour** (1006 Mendocino Ave., Santa Rosa, CA 95401, tel. 707/546–9888 or 800/225–5759, fax 707/546–9891, www.skylinktravel.com), serving lesbian travelers.

Holidays

All government and post offices, banks, and most shops are closed in Belgium on Belgium's national day, July 21. Businesses are also closed on Easter Monday, Labor Day (May 1), the Ascension (May), Pentecost (June), the Assumption (August), All Saints Day (early November), Armistice Day (November 11), Christmas Day, and New Years Day. If a holiday falls on a weekend, offices close the preceding Friday or following Monday.

Language

Belgium has three official languages: Flemish, French, and German (spoken by a small minority). Many Flemish-speaking Belgians understand French and vice versa. Nonetheless, Belgians are often uncomfortable using the other region's language, and many are capable and more than willing to speak English, especially to anglophones. So, **speak the language of the region if you know it, or use English.**

Lodging

Brussels offers a range of lodging, from the major international hotel chains and small, modern local hotels to family-run restored inns and historic houses to elegant country châteaux and resorts.

Most hotels that cater to business travelers will grant substantial weekend rebates. These discounted rates are often available during the week as well as in July and early August, when business travelers are thin on the ground. Moreover, you can often qualify for a "corporate rate" when hotel occupancy is low. The moral is, always ask what's the best rate a hotel can offer before you book. No hotelier was ever born who will give a lower rate unless you ask for it.

The lodgings we list are the cream of the crop in each price category. We always list the facilities that are available—but we don't specify whether they cost extra: when pricing accommodations, always ask what's included and what costs extra.

Assume that hotels operate on the **European Plan** (with no meals) unless we specify that they use the **Continental Plan** (CP, with a Continental breakfast), **Modified American Plan** (MAP, with breakfast and dinner), or the **Full American Plan** (FAP, with all meals).

➤ RESERVATIONS: For hotel reservations in Belgium (a free service): **Belgian Tourist Reservations** (BTR; Bd. Anspach 111, 1000 Brussels, tel. 02/513–7484, fax 02/513–9277).

HOSTELS

No matter what your age, you can **save on lodging costs by staying at hostels.** Hostels in Belgium are well organized and clean. Rooms with 1–10 beds are available and hostels are suitable for family stays. Many are conveniently located near train stations.

In some 5,000 locations in more than 70 countries around the world, Hostelling International (HI), the umbrella group for a number of national youth-hostel associations, offers single-sex, dorm-style beds and, at many hostels, rooms for couples and family accommodations. Membership in any HI national hostel association, open to travelers of all ages, allows you to stay in HI-affiliated hostels at member rates; one-year membership is about $25 for adults (C$26.75 in Canada, £9.30 in the U.K., $30 in Australia, and $30 in New Zealand); hostels run about $10–$25 per night. Members have priority if the hostel is full; they're also eligible for discounts around the world, even on rail and bus travel in some countries.

➤ BEST OPTIONS: **Auberges de Jeunesse de la Belgique Francophone** (Rue de la Sablonnière 28, 1000 Brussels, tel. 02/219–5676, fax 02/219–1451).

➤ ORGANIZATIONS: **Hostelling International—American Youth Hostels** (733 15th St. NW, Suite 840, Washington, DC 20005, tel. 202/783–6161, fax 202/783–6171, www.hiayh.org). **Hostelling International—Canada** (400–205 Catherine St., Ottawa, Ontario K2P 1C3, tel. 613/237–7884, fax 613/237–7868, www.hostellingintl.ca). **Youth Hostel Association of England and Wales** (Trevelyan House, 8 St. Stephen's Hill, St. Albans, Hertfordshire AL1 2DY, tel. 01727/855215 or 01727/845047, fax 01727/844126, www.yha.uk). **Australian Youth Hostel Association** (10 Mallett St., Camperdown, NSW 2050, tel. 02/9565–1699, fax 02/9565–1325, www.yha.com.au). **Youth Hostels Association of New Zealand** (Box 436, Christchurch, New Zealand, tel. 03/379–9970, fax 03/365–4476, www.yha.org.nz).

HOTELS

Hotels in Brussels are rated with stars, one star indicating the most basic and five stars indicating the most luxurious. Rooms in one-star hotels are likely not to have a telephone or television, and two-star hotels may not have carpeting, air-conditioning, or elevators. Four- and five-star hotels have conference facilities and offer amenities such as pools, tennis courts, saunas, private parking, and room service.

Three-, four-, and five-star hotels are usually equipped with hair dryers and coffeemakers. Hotels in Belgium do not provide irons, although four- and five-star hotels offer dry-cleaning service. Most hotels have at least one restaurant.

All hotels listed in this book have private bath unless otherwise noted. Single rooms in one- to three-star hotels often have a shower (*douche* in French, *stortbui* in Flemish) rather than a bathtub (*bain* in French, *badkuip* in Flemish). A double room includes either one double bed (*lit double* in French, *tweepersoonsbed* in Flemish) or two single beds. A single room includes one single bed (*lit simple* in French or *eenpersoonsbed* in Flemish). Three people who wish to room together should **ask about the possibility of adding a small bed in a double room.** Rooms that accommodate four people are rare, except in five-star hotels.

Taking meals at the hotel restaurant usually provides you with a discount. Some restaurants, especially country inns, require that guests take half-board (*demi-pension* in French, *half-pension* in Flemish), at least lunch or dinner, at the hotel. Full pension (*Pension complet* in French, *volledig pension* in Flemish) entitles guests to both lunch and dinner. Guests taking either half or full board also receive breakfast. If you take a *pension*, you pay per person, regardless of the number of rooms. If you are not taking half or full pension, **ask if breakfast is included in the price of the room.**

Metro, Tram, and Bus

The metro, trams, and buses operate as part of the same system. All three are clean and efficient, and a single ticket, which can be used on all three, costs BF50/€1.25. The best buy is a 10-trip ticket, which costs BF350/€8.70, or a one-day card costing BF140/€3.45. You need to stamp your ticket in the appropriate machine on the bus or tram; in the metro, your card is stamped as you pass through the automatic barrier. You can purchase these tickets in any metro station or at newsstands. Single tickets can be purchased on the bus or on the tram.

Detailed maps of the Brussels public transportation network are available in most metro stations and at the Tourist Information Brussels in the Grand'Place (☞ see Visitor Information *below*). You get a map free with a Tourist Passport (also available at the tourist office), which, for BF300/€7.40, allows you a one-day transport card and reductions at museums.

Money Matters

Prices throughout this guide are given for adults. Substantially reduced fees are almost always available for children, students, and senior citizens. For information on taxes, *see* Taxes, *below*.

ATMS

ATMs (*distributeur automatique* in French, *automatisch uitdeler* in Flemish) are located at banks in Brussels, either inside the bank itself or on the facade of the bank building. They are accessible 24 hours a day, seven days per week, but are occasionally guarded and inaccessible, usually for about an hour, when cash is being transferred from the machines. The distributors themselves determine with which networks they work. For example, BBL works with Maestro, General Bank also works with Maestro and Cirrus, and CGER-ASLK works with Maestro, Cirrus, and Plus. To be sure, **inquire at your home bank** about use of its network in Brussels.

CREDIT CARDS

Major credit cards are excepted in most hotels, gas stations, and restaurants in Brussels. Smaller establishments, shops, and supermarkets often accept Visa cards only.

Throughout this guide, the following abbreviations are used: **AE,** American Express; **DC,** Diners Club; **MC,** Master Card; and **V,** Visa.

➤ REPORTING LOST CARDS: To report lost or stolen credit cards, call the following toll-free numbers: **American Express** (tel. 800/327–2177); **Diner's Club** (tel. 800/234–6377); **Master Card** (tel. 800/307–7309); and **Visa** (tel. 800/847–2911).

In Belgium, use the following numbers: **American Express** (tel. 02/676-2626). **Diner's Club** (tel. 02/206-9800). **Master Card/ Visa** (tel. 070/344-344).

CURRENCY

The monetary unit in Belgium is the Belgian franc (BF). The currency exchange rates fluctuate daily, so check them at the time of your departure.

As a member of the European Union, Belgium adopted the European currency, the euro, in January 1999, and since then it has been possible to make banking transactions in euros as well as in the local currency. As of January 1, 2002, all bank transactions must be made in euros, and euro coins and banknotes will replace the coins and notes of the local currency.

CURRENCY EXCHANGE

Currency exchange booths are widely available throughout Brussels, at major train stations, and at major tourist destinations. There is a surcharge for each transaction, regardless of the amount exchanged.

For the most favorable rates, **change money through banks.** Although ATM transaction fees may be higher abroad than at home, ATM rates are excellent because they are based on wholesale rates offered only by major banks. You won't do as well at exchange booths in airports or rail and bus stations, in hotels, in restaurants, or in stores. To avoid lines at airport exchange booths, **get a bit of local currency before you leave home.**

➤ EXCHANGE SERVICES: **International Currency Express** (tel. 888/ 278-6628 for orders, www.foreignmoney.com). **Thomas Cook Currency Services** (tel. 800/287-7362 for telephone orders and retail locations, www.us.thomascook.com).

Packing

The best advice for a trip to Brussels in any season is to pack light, be flexible, bring an umbrella (and trench coat with a liner

150

in winter), and always have a sweater or jacket available. For daytime wear and casual evenings, turtlenecks and flannel shirts are ideal for winter, alone or under a sweater, and cotton shirts with sleeves are perfect in summer. Blue jeans are popular and are even sometimes worn to the office; sweat suits, however, are never seen outside fitness centers. For women, high heels are nothing but trouble on the cobblestone streets of Brussels and other old cities, and sneakers or running shoes are a dead giveaway that you are an American tourist; a better choice is a pair of dark-color walking shoes or low-heeled pumps.

Women here wear skirts more frequently than do women in the United States, especially those over 35. Men would be wise to include a jacket and tie, especially if you're planning to visit one of the upper-echelon restaurants.

Passports & Visas

All Australian, Canadian, New Zealand, U.K., and U.S. citizens, even infants, need a valid passport to enter Belgium for stays of up to 90 days.

➤ AUSTRALIAN CITIZENS: **Australian Passport Office** (tel. 131–232, www.dfat.gov.au/passports).

➤ CANADIAN CITIZENS: **Passport Office** (tel. 819/994–3500 or 800/567–6868, www.dfait-maeci.gc.ca/passport).

➤ NEW ZEALAND CITIZENS: **New Zealand Passport Office** (tel. 04/494–0700, www.passports.govt.nz).

➤ U.K. CITIZENS: **London Passport Office** (tel. 0990/210–410) for fees and documentation requirements and to request an emergency passport.

➤ U.S. CITIZENS: **National Passport Information Center** (tel. 900/225–5674; calls are 35¢ per minute for automated service, $1.05 per minute for operator service).

Rest Rooms

Public rest rooms (*Toilettes* in French, *Toiletten* in Flemish) are also referred to as *WC*. There are no free public rest rooms in cities or at rest stops on highways. Train stations, tourist spots, beaches, and highway restaurants have rest rooms manned by attendants who charge about 15 francs per visit. Payment is made on the way out. Thanks to the attendant, these rest rooms are clean and equipped with toilet paper. Similarly, restaurants in cities often hire attendants who charge per visit. **Expect to pay, even if you are a patron of the restaurant.**

Rest rooms in cafés and pubs are not manned by attendants and are free to patrons. Therefore, even if your visit to a café is expressly to use the rest room, you are expected to buy a drink. If you do not have the time or inclination to drink, ask first before using the rest room in cafés. Offering the bartender 15 francs for the hospitality is a fair gesture.

Gas stations along highways usually have a unisex rest room. For access you need not buy gas, just **ask the gas station attendant for the key.** Rest rooms in cafés, bars, and gas stations are often not up to the same standards as those manned by attendants, so **take tissues with you.**

Safety

Brussels is relatively safe, even at night. Nontheless, it is wise to **avoid highway rest stops and sparsely populated metro stations at night.** Although they are not likely to assault, tramps and derelicts tend to make train stations unsavory at night.

Beware of pickpockets, especially around tourist attractions, in public transportation, and in the airport. Even in restaurants, particularly those in tourist areas, keep an eye on your handbag or wallet. **Lock your car.** Do not expect a great deal of sympathy if you have been pickpocketed or burglarized. Local police make reports but usually investigate no further.

Shopping

Shopping in Belgium can be expensive, but goods are of the finest quality. You can find lace, tapestries, linen, chocolate, crystal, and porcelain near the Grand'Place in Brussels and at the airport. If you make a significant purchase, **ask about a discount.**

Art galleries and antiques shops are plentiful in Brussels. *Antiquaire* shops deal with bona fide antiques. If you are simply looking for interesting, older "vintage" items, visit a *brocante* or look for street sales organized, usually in May and September, by villages and neighborhoods.

Bargaining is expected at antiques shops, brocantes, and street sales. Depending on the volume of your purchase, you can usually trim your price by 10% to 35%. If you are not satisfied with the price quoted and wish to be taken seriously, **walk away and then visit the vendor later for another chance to bargain.**

Belgium's largest department store, INNO, found in major cities and shopping centers, stocks a wide variety of quality clothing and housewares. Less expensive are hypermarkets GB-Maxi and Cora, located on the cities' outskirts. In January and July these shops and most others put their goods on sale, often with reductions of 50%.

Sightseeing Guides

English-language sightseeing tours are routinely organized in Brussels. You can find information about reliable tours, guides, and schedules through national tourism offices (☞ Visitor Information, *below*). Museums and special exhibits often offer English-language guides or headphones with explanations in English.

ARAU organizes thematic city bus and walking tours from March through November, including "Brussels 1900: Art Nouveau" and "Brussels 1930: Art Deco." Tours include visits to some building interiors that are otherwise not open to the public. The cost is BF600/€14.80 for a half-day coach tour and BF300/€7.40 for a half-day walking tour. The original tours run by Chatterbus, from early June through September either visit the main sights on foot or by minibus (BF600/€14.80), or follow a walking route that includes a visit to a bistro (BF250/€6.20). De Boeck Sightseeing operates city tours (BF800/€19.80) with multilingual cassette commentary; they also visit Antwerp, the Ardennes, Brugge, Gent, Ieper, and Waterloo. Passengers are picked up at major hotels or at the tourist office in the town hall. Pro Velo takes visitors on themed cycling tours in and around Brussels. Tours, on themes including "The Heart of Brussels Through the Centuries" and "Comic Strips and Cafès," are available from April through August. Tours in English operate in July and August. The cost is BF300/€7.40, plus BF200/€4.95 for bike rental. Group tours can also be arranged throughout the year at a cost of BF5,000/€124 for up to 20 people for a half-day tour, plus BF200/€4.95 per person for bike rental. Bikes may also be rented for independent use at prices ranging from BF100/€2.50 for one hour to BF2,000/€49.50 for a full week.

Qualified guides are available for individual tours from the Tourist Information Brussels in the town hall. Three hours costs BF3,200/€79.50, and up to 25 people can share the same guide for a walking tour and up to 50 people for a bus tour.

In Waterloo expert guides, Les Guides 1815, can be hired to take you around the battlefield for one hour (BF1,400/€34.50) and three hours (BF2,200/€54.50); group tours in English (BF100/€2.50 per person) are weekends at 4, July through August.

➤ CONTACTS: **ARAU** (Bd. Adolphe Max 55, tel. 02/219–3345). **Chatterbus** (R. des Thuyas 12, tel. 02/673–1835. **De Boeck Sightseeing** (R. de la Colline 8, Grand'Place, tel. 02/513–7744). **Les Guides 1815** (Rte. du Lion 250, tel. 02/385–0625). **Pro Velo** (R. de Londres 15, tel. 02/502–7355). **Tourist Information Brussels** (TIB; tel. 02/513–8940).

Students in Brussels

Students or young people under 26 can benefit from many discounts, including public transportation, museum entrances, cultural events, and even discount haircuts at some stylists. Be sure to **take your student ID and government identification** with your date of birth.

➤ IDs & Services: **Council Travel** (CIEE; 205 E. 42nd St., 14th floor, New York, NY 10017, tel. 212/822–2700 or 888/268–6245, fax 212/822–2699, www.councilexchanges.org) for mail orders only, in the U.S. **Travel Cuts** (187 College St., Toronto, Ontario M5T 1P7, tel. 416/979–2406 or 800/667–2887, www.travelcuts.com) in Canada. **Carte Jeunes** (Rue des Mineurs 16, Liège Belgium, tel. 04/221–3355, fax 04/221–0621).

Taxes

AIRPORT

The Brussels National Airport tax is BF525/13.00, levied on all tickets and payable with your ticket purchase.

HOTELS

All hotels in Belgium charge a 6% Value Added Tax (TVA), included in the room rate; in Brussels, there is also a 9% city tax.

VALUE-ADDED TAX

In Belgium, VAT ranges from 6% on food and clothing to 33% on luxury goods. Restaurants are in between; 21% VAT is included in quoted prices.

To get a VAT refund you need to reside outside the European Union and to have spent 5,001 Belgian francs (125) or more in the same shop on the same day. Provided that you personally carry the goods out of the country within 30 days, you may claim a refund. Systems for doing this vary. Most leading stores will issue you a "VAT cheque" as proof of purchase (and charge a commission for the service). Then have these tax-refund forms stamped at customs as you leave the final European Union country on your itinerary; send the stamped form back to the store. Alternatively, if you shop at a store that is part of the Global Refund program, you can simplify the process.

Global Refund is a VAT refund service that makes getting your money back hassle-free. The service is available Europe-wide at 130,000 affiliated stores. In participating stores, **ask for the Global Refund form** (called a Shopping Cheque). Have it stamped like any customs form by customs officials when you leave the European Union. Then take the form to one of the more than 700 Global Refund counters—conveniently located at every major airport and border crossing—and your money will be refunded on the spot in the form of cash, check, or a refund to your credit-card account (minus a small percentage for processing).

➤ **VAT REFUNDS: Global Refund** (707 Summer St., Stamford, CT 06901, tel. 800/566–9828, fax 203/674–8709, www. globalrefund.com).

Taxis

Call Taxis Verts or Taxis Oranges. You can also catch one at cab stands around town. Distances are not great, and a cab ride costs between BF250/€6.20 and BF500/€12.40. Tips are included in the fare.

➤ **TAXI COMPANIES: Taxis Oranges** (tel. 02/349–4343). **Taxis Verts** (tel. 02/349–4949).

Telephones

Telephone lines in Belgium are modern and efficient. Phone numbers have nine digits: either a six-digit local number preceded by a three-digit area code, or a seven-digit local number preceded by a two-digit area code. Cell phones are called GSMs. British cell phones work in Belgium, but American and Canadian cells phones do not. Cell phone telephone numbers are preceded by 075, 077, 095, or 097, followed by six digits.

AREA & COUNTRY CODES

The country code (used when calling from abroad) for Belgium is 32. The two- or three-digit area code (called a city code when applied to metropolitan areas) will always begin with zero; the zero is dropped when calling from abroad. The city code for Brussels is 02.

The country code for the United States and Canada is 1. The country code is 61 for Australia, 64 for New Zealand, 44 for the United Kingdom, and 353 for Ireland.

DIRECTORY & OPERATOR ASSISTANCE

For English-language telephone assistance, dial 1405.

INTERNATIONAL CALLS

For international calls, dial 00, followed by the country code, followed by the area code and telephone number.

LOCAL CALLS

Use the city code (02) for all calls within Brussels, followed by the seven-digit local number. Unlike in the United States, the cost of local calls in Belgium increases depending upon the duration of the call.

LONG-DISTANCE CALLS

If your are making a call from city to city within Belgium, the number you dial will have a total of nine digits, either a two-digit area code and a seven-digit local number or a three-digit area code and a six-digit local number.

LONG-DISTANCE SERVICES

Avoid making lengthy long-distance telephone calls directly from your hotel room, as hefty surplus charges are added. Instead use a phone card (☞ *below*) or use a long-distance provider.

AT&T, MCI, and Sprint access codes make calling long distance relatively convenient, but you may find the local access number blocked in many hotel rooms. First ask the hotel operator to connect you. If the hotel operator balks, ask for an international operator, or dial the international operator yourself. One way to improve your odds of getting connected to your long-distance carrier is to travel with more than one company's calling card (a hotel may block Sprint, for example, but not MCI). If all else fails, call from a pay phone.

➤ ACCESS CODES: **AT&T Direct** (tel. 080010010 Belgium; 800/435–0812 other areas). **MCI WorldPhone** (tel. 080010012 Belgium; 800/444–4141 other areas). **Sprint International Access** (tel. 080010014 Belgium; 800/877–7746 other areas).

PHONE CARDS

Most coin-operated public telephones in Belgium have been replaced by card-operated phones. Telephone cards are sold at post offices, newspaper stands, and many train stations. The minimum card costs 200 Belgian francs (4.95).

PUBLIC PHONES

Most public pay phones require a telephone card (☞ Phone Cards, *above*). Those that still accept coins require BF20 or Flux 20 for a three-minute call. After the dial tone, pay with either your telephone card or with coins, then dial your number.

Tipping

In Belgium, a tip (*service compris* or *service inclusief*) is always included in restaurant and hotel bills and in taxi fares. Railway porters expect BF30/€0.75 per item on weekdays and BF40/€1.00 per item on weekends. For bellhops and doormen, BF100/€2.50 is adequate. Give movie ushers BF20/€0.50 per person in your party, whether or not they show you to your seat. And tip doormen at bars, nightclubs, or discos at least BF50/€1.25 if you're planning to go back.

Train Travel

Eurostar trains from London (Waterloo) use the Channel Tunnel to cut travel time to Brussels (Gare du Midi) to 2 hours, 40 minutes. Trains stop at Ashford (Kent) and Lille (France). At press time there were 11 daily services, and a first-class, one-way ticket cost BF9,500/€235; second-class tickets cost BF6,500/€160 (weekdays) or BF4,250/€105 (weekends). Promotional fares are available but must be booked seven days in advance.

Brussels is linked with Paris, Amsterdam, and Liège by Thalys high-speed trains. On the new Thalys high-speed trains, a one-way ticket from Brussels to Paris costs about $90 in first class and $60 in economy. The trip lasts 85 minutes. Reserved seats are obligatory for both Eurostar and Thalys trains. In Holland, until new tracks have been laid (scheduled for 2005), they provide a slower but very comfortable ride of just over 3 hours.

Conventional train services from London connect with the Ramsgate–Oostende ferry, hovercraft, or catamaran, and from Oostende the train takes you to Brussels. The whole journey, using hovercraft or catamaran, takes about 6½ hours; by ferry, about 9 hours. For more information, contact Connex South-Eastern or the British Tourist Authority. Belgian National Railways is the national rail line.

There is frequent commuter train service from Brussels to Waterloo.

CLASSES

Train travel is available in first or second class. First-class seats are slightly more spacious and are upholstered. First-class passengers on Thalys trips to Paris are served a light meal and beverage.

High-speed trains, intercity trains, and local trains alike offer smoking or no-smoking sections.

FARES & SCHEDULES

Major train stations have an information office for information about fares and schedules. All train stations post complete listings, by time, of arrivals and departures, including the track number.

To avoid crowds, don't travel by train to the Belgian coast on Saturday morning or return from there on Sunday afternoon in the summer. Belgium's national holiday, July 21, also draws train travelers from Brussels to the seaside and the Ardennes.

➤ TRAIN INFORMATION: **Belgian National Railways** (SNCB, tel. 02/555–2525). **British Tourist Authority** (Av. Louise 306, B1050 Brussels, tel. 02/646–3510). **Brussels Train Station** (tel. 02/555–2555). **Connex South-Eastern** (tel. 870/603–0405).

PAYING

Train tickets bought in Belgium can be paid for using currency or a major credit card—American Express, Diners Club, Master Card, or Visa. You cannot pay for train tickets with traveler's checks, but currency exchange booths in the stations can cash your checks. For international travel, you may pay and reserve with a credit card by telephone, at the train station itself, or through a local travel agency.

RESERVATIONS

Reservations are obligatory on the Eurostar train to London and on the Thalys train to Paris. Reservations are not required for domestic trains or for trains between Brussels and Luxembourg City. For further information contact the Brussels train station (☞ Fares and Schedules, *above*).

➤ CONTACTS: **Eurostar** (tel. 0900/10–366; 0900/10–177). **Thalys** (tel. 0900–10–177; 0800/95–777).

Transportation around Brussels

In Brussels, public transportation by tram, metro, and bus is not as frequent or easy to master as in London or Paris. Taxis are available at major train stations, and fares within the city are reasonable. Fares increase dramatically once you travel outside city limits.

Travel Agencies

A good travel agent puts your needs first. Look for an agency that has been in business at least five years, emphasizes customer service, and has someone on staff who specializes in your destination. In addition, **make sure the agency belongs to a professional trade organization.** The American Society of Travel Agents (ASTA), with 27,000 agents in some 170 countries, is the largest and most influential in the field. Operating under the motto "Integrity in Travel," it maintains and enforces a strict code of ethics and will step in to help mediate any agent-client disputes if necessary. ASTA also maintains a Web site that includes a directory of agents. (If a travel agency is also acting as your tour operator, *see* Buyer Beware *in* Tours & Packages, *above*.)

➤ LOCAL AGENT REFERRALS: **American Society of Travel Agents** (ASTA; tel. 800/965–2782 24-hr hot line, fax 703/684–8319, www.astanet.com). **Association of British Travel Agents** (68–71 Newman St., London W1P 4AH, tel. 0171/637–2444, fax 0171/637–0713, www.abtanet.com). **Association of Canadian Travel Agents** (1729 Bank St., Suite 201, Ottawa, Ontario K1V 7Z5, tel. 613/521–0474, fax 613/521–0805). **Australian Federation of Travel Agents** (Level 3, 309 Pitt St., Sydney 2000, tel. 02/9264–3299, fax 02/9264–1085, www.afta.com.au). **Travel Agents' Association of New Zealand** (Box 1888, Wellington 10033, tel. 04/499–0104, fax 04/499–0827).

➤ LOCAL AGENCIES: **American Express** (Houtweg 24, tel. 02/245–2250). **Carlson/Wagonlit Travel** (Bd. Clovis, tel. 02/287–8811).

Visitor Information

➤ BELGIAN NATIONAL TOURIST OFFICE: **In the U.S.:** 780 3rd Ave., New York, NY 10017, tel. 212/758–8130, fax 212/355–7675. **In Canada:** Box 760 NDG, Montréal, Québec H4A 3S2, tel. 514/484–3594, fax 514/489–8965. **In the U.K.:** 29 Princes St., London W1R 7RG, tel. 0171/629–0230, fax 0171/629–0454.

➤ **WITHIN BELGIUM: Belgian Office of Tourism** (61-63, rue Marché aux Herbes, 1000 Brussels, tel. 02/513–6950, fax 02/513–8803). **Tourist Information Brussels** (TIB; Hôtel de Ville/Grand' Place, tel. 02/513–8940). **Waterloo Office de Tourisme** (tourist office; Chaussée de Bruxelles 149, tel. 02/354–9910).

➤ **U.S. GOVERNMENT ADVISORIES: U.S. Department of State** (Overseas Citizens Services Office, Room 4811 N.S., 2201 C St. NW, Washington, DC 20520, tel. 202/647–5225 for interactive hot line; 301/946–4400 for computer bulletin board; fax 202/647–3000 for interactive hot line); enclose a self-addressed, stamped, business-size envelope.

Web Sites

Do check out the World Wide Web when you're planning. You'll find everything from current weather forecasts to virtual tours of famous cities. Fodor's Web site, www.fodors.com, is a great place to start your on-line travels.

For more information specifically on Belgium, visit www.Belgium. fgov.be, www.toervl.be, www.opt.be, www.hotels-belgium.com, and www.belgium-tourism.net.

Railway Web sites are as follows: Belgian Railway, www.b-rail. be; Thalys, www.thalys.com; Eurostar, www.sncb.be

When to Go

The best times to visit these two countries are in the late spring—when the northern European days are long and the summer crowds have not yet filled the beaches, the highways, or the museums—and in fall.

Because Belgians take vacations in July and August, these months are not ideal for visiting the coast or the Ardennes, but summer is a very good time to be in Brussels. In summer you will also be able to get a break on hotel prices; on the other hand, this is also vacation time for many restaurants. For touring the country and visiting much-frequented tourist attractions, the best times are April–June and September–October.

CLIMATE

What follows are average daily maximum and minimum temperatures in Brussels.

➤ FORECASTS: WEATHER CHANNEL CONNECTION (TEL. 900/932–8437), 95¢ PER MINUTE FROM A TOUCH-TONE PHONE.

BRUSSELS

Jan.	40F	4C	May	65F	18C	Sept.	70F	21C
	31	−1		47	8		52	11
Feb.	45F	7C	June	72F	22C	Oct.	59F	15C
	32	0		52	11		45	7
Mar.	50F	10C	July	74F	23C	Nov.	49F	9C
	36	2		54	12		38	3
Apr.	58F	14C	Aug.	72F	22C	Dec.	43F	6C
	41	5		54	12		34	1

DUTCH VOCABULARY

ENGLISH	DUTCH	PRONUNCIATION

Basics

Yes/no	Ja, nee	yah, nay
Please	Alstublieft	**ahls**-too-bleeft
Thank you	Dank u	**dahnk** oo
You're welcome	Niets te danken	neets teh **dahn**-ken
Excuse me, sorry	Pardon	pahr-**don**
Good morning	Goede morgen	**hoh**-deh **mor**-ghen
Good evening	Goede avond	**hoh**-deh **ahv**-unt
Goodbye	Dag!	dah

Numbers

one	een	ehn
two	twee	tveh
three	drie	dree
four	vier	veer
five	vijf	vehf
six	zes	zehss
seven	zeven	**zeh**-vehn
eight	acht	ahkht
nine	negen	**neh**-ghen
ten	tien	teen

Days of the Week

Sunday	zondag	**zohn**-dagh
Monday	maandag	**mahn**-dagh
Tuesday	dinsdag	**dinns**-dagh
Wednesday	woensdag	**voons**-dagh
Thursday	donderdag	**don**-der-dagh
Friday	vrijdag	**vreh**-dagh
Saturday	zaterdag	**zah**-ter-dagh

Useful Phrases

Do you speak English?	Spreekt U Engels?	sprehkt oo **ehn**-gls
I don't speak Dutch	Ik spreek geen Nederlands	ihk sprehk **ghen Ned**-er-lahnds
I don't understand	Ik begrijp het niet	ihk be-**ghrehp** het neet
I don't know	Ik weet niet	ihk **veht** ut neet
I'm American/ English	Ik ben Amerikaans/ Engels	ihk ben Am-er-ee-**kahns**/Ehn-gls
Where is . . .	Waar is . . .	vahr iss
the train station?	het station?	heht stah-**syohn**
the post office?	het postkantoor?	het **pohst**-kahn-tohr
the hospital?	het ziekenhuis?	het **zeek**-uhn-haus
Where are the restrooms?	waar is de WC?	vahr iss de **veh**-seh
Left/right	links/rechts	leenks/rehts
How much is this?	Hoeveel kost dit?	hoo-**vehl** kohst deet
It's expensive/ cheap	Het is te duur/ goedkoop	het ees teh **dour**/ **hood**-kohp
I am ill/sick	Ik ben ziek	ihk behn zeek
I want to call a doctor	Ik wil een docter bellen	ihk veel ehn **dohk**-ter **behl**-len
Help!	Help!	help
Stop!	Stoppen!	**stop**-pen

Dining Out

Bill/check	de rekening	de **rehk**-en-eeng
Bread	brood	brohd
Butter	boter	**boh**-ter
Fork	vork	fork
I'd like to order	Ik wil graag bestellen	Ihk veel khrah behs-**tell**-en
Knife	een mes	ehn mehs
Menu	menu/kaart	men-**oo**/kahrt

Napkin	en servet	ehn ser-**veht**
Pepper	peper	**peh**-per
Please give	mag ik	mahkh ihk
me . . .	[een] . . .	[ehn] . . .
Salt	zout	zoot
Spoon	een lepel	ehn **leh**-pehl
Sugar	suiker	**sigh**-kur

FRENCH VOCABULARY

| ENGLISH | FRENCH | PRONUNCIATION |

Basics

Yes/no	Oui/non	wee/no
Please	S'il vous plaît	seel voo play
Thank you	Merci	mare-**see**
You're welcome	De rien	deh ree-**en**
Excuse me, sorry	Pardon	pahr-**doan**
Good morning/ afternoon	Bonjour	bone-**joor**
Good evening	Bonsoir	bone-**swar**
Goodbye	Au revoir	o ruh-**vwar**

Numbers

one	un	un
two	deux	dew
three	trois	twa
four	quatre	**cat**-ruh
five	cinq	sank
six	six	seess
seven	sept	set
eight	huit	wheat
nine	neuf	nuf
ten	dix	deess

Days of the Week

Sunday	dimanche	dee-**mahnsh**
Monday	lundi	lewn-**dee**
Tuesday	mardi	mar-**dee**
Wednesday	mercredi	mare-kruh-**dee**
Thursday	jeudi	juh-**dee**
Friday	vendredi	van-dra-**dee**
Saturday	samedi	sam-**dee**

Useful Phrases

Do you speak English?	Parlez-vous anglais?	**par**-lay vooz ahng-**glay**
I don't speak French	Je ne parle pas français	jeh nuh parl pah fraun-**say**
I don't understand	Je ne comprends pas	jeh nuh kohm-prahn **pah**
I don't know	Je ne sais pas	jeh nuh say **pah**
I'm American/British	Je suis américain/anglais	jeh sweez a-may-ree-**can**/ahng-**glay**
Where is . . . the train station? the post office? the hospital?	Où est . . . la gare? la poste? l'hôpital?	oo ay la gar la post low-pee-**tahl**
Where are the restrooms?	Où sont les toilettes?	oo son lay twah-**let**
Left/right	A gauche/à droite	a goash/a drwat
How much is it? It's expensive/cheap	C'est combien? C'est cher/pas cher	say comb-bee-**en** say sher/pa sher
I am ill/sick	Je suis malade	jeh swee ma-**lahd**
Call a doctor	Appelez un docteur	a-pe-lay un dohk-**tore**
Help!	Au secours!	o say-**koor**
Stop!	Arrêtez!	a-ruh-**tay**

Dining Out

Bill/check	l'addition	la-dee-see-**own**
Bread	du pain	due pan
Butter	du beurre	due bur
Fork	une fourchette	ewn four-**shet**
I'd like . . .	Je voudrais . . .	jeh voo-**dray**
Knife	un couteau	un koo-**toe**
Menu	la carte	la cart
Napkin	une serviette	ewn sair-vee-**et**
Pepper	du poivre	due **pwah**-vruh
Salt	du sel	dew sell
Spoon	une cuillère	ewn kwee-**air**
Sugar	du sucre	due **sook**-ruh

INDEX

184

FODOR'S POCKET BRUSSELS

EDITORS: Matt Lombardi, Holly S. Smith, Kirsten Weisenberger

EDITORIAL CONTRIBUTORS: Leslie Adler, Eric R. Dorsin, Barbara Jacobs, Katharine Mill

EDITORIAL PRODUCTION: Stacey Kulig

MAPS: David Lindroth, *cartographer*; Bob Blake and Rebecca Baer, *map editors*

DESIGN: Fabrizio La Rocca, *creative director*; Tigist Getachew, *art director*; Melanie Marin, *photo editor*

PRODUCTION/MANUFACTURING: Angela L. McLean

COVER PHOTOGRAPH: Charles & Josette Lenars/Corbis

COPYRIGHT

1st Edition

ISBN 0–679–00781–4

ISSN 1533–9343

IMPORTANT TIP

Although all prices, opening times, and other details in this book are based on information supplied to us at press time, changes occur all the time in the travel world, and Fodor's cannot accept responsibility for facts that become outdated or for inadvertent errors or omissions. So **always confirm information when it matters,** especially if you're making a detour to visit a specific place.

SPECIAL SALES

PRINTED IN THE UNITED STATES OF AMERICA

10 9 8 7 6 5 4 3 2 1